STUDENT'S
with Interact

CEFR
A2

SECOND EDITION

Herbert Puchta,
Jeff Stranks &
Peter Lewis-Jones

CAMBRIDGE
University Press

CONTENTS

Welcome p 4 **A** Personal information; Nationalities and *be*; Names and addresses **B** Things in the classroom; Prepositions of place; Classroom language; Object pronouns; *this / that / these / those* **C** Days and dates; My day **D** My possessions; *have got*; *I like* and *I'd like*

	FUNCTIONS & SPEAKING	GRAMMAR	VOCABULARY
Unit 1 **Having a good time** p 12	Talking about routines and everyday activities Expressing likes and dislikes Giving warnings and stating prohibition Developing Speaking: Talking about free time activities	Present simple review ▶ *like* + *-ing* Adverbs of frequency	Hobbies **WordWise**: Collocations with *have*
Unit 2 **Spending money** p 20	Role play: Buying things in a shop Talking about what people are doing at the moment	Present continuous ▶ Verbs of perception Present simple vs. present continuous	Shops Clothes

Life Competencies: Empathy ▶, **Culture:** Banknotes around the world ▶, Review

Unit 3 **We are what we eat** p 30	Talking about food Ordering a meal Developing Speaking: Apologising	▶ Countable and uncountable nouns *a/an, some, any* (*how*) *much* / *many, a lot of* / *lots of* *too* and (*not*) *enough*	Food and drink **WordWise**: Expressions with *have got* Adjectives to talk about food
Unit 4 **All in the family** p 38	Talking about families Asking for permission	Possessive adjectives and pronouns *whose* and possessive *'s* ▶ *was* / *were*	Family members Feelings

Life Competencies: Saying sorry ▶, **Culture:** Family traditions around the world ▶, Review

Unit 5 **No place like home** p 48	Talking about events in the past Role play: At a market Developing Speaking: Making and responding to suggestions	Past simple (regular verbs) Modifiers: *quite, very, really* ▶ Past simple (negative)	Parts of a house and furniture **WordWise**: Phrasal verbs with *look* Adjectives with *-ed* or *-ing*
Unit 6 **Friends forever** p 56	Saying what you like doing with others Talking about friends and friendships Talking about past events	Past simple (irregular verbs) Double genitive ▶ Past simple questions	Past time expressions Personality adjectives

Life Competencies: Be careful making judgments ▶, **Culture:** Friends in literature ▶, Review

Unit 7 **Smart life** p 66	Giving advice Talking about obligation / lack of obligation Role play: A phone call Developing Speaking: Asking for repetition and clarification	*have to* / *don't have to* *should* / *shouldn't* ▶ *mustn't* vs. *don't have to*	Gadgets **WordWise**: Expressions with *like* Housework
Unit 8 **A question of sport** p 74	Talking about sports Talking about feelings Talking about ongoing past events, sequencing events	Past continuous ▶ Past continuous vs. past simple *when* and *while*	Sport and sports verbs Adverbs of sequence

Life Competencies: Solving problems ▶, **Culture:** The wonderful world of sport ▶, Review

Unit 9 **Wild and wonderful** p 84	Talking about the weather Developing Speaking: Paying compliments	Comparative adjectives ▶ *can* / *can't* (for ability) Superlative adjectives	Geographical features **WordWise**: Phrases with *with* The weather
Unit 10 **Out and about** p 92	Talking about plans Inviting and making arrangements Discussing ideas for an imaginary film	▶ *be going to* for intentions Present continuous for arrangements Adverbs	Places in town Things in town: compound nouns

Life Competencies: Helping in the community ▶, **Culture:** Mythical places around the world ▶, Review

Unit 11 **Future bodies** p 102	Making predictions Role play: At the doctor's Developing Speaking: Sympathising with people	*will* / *won't* for future predictions ▶ First conditional Time clauses with *when* / *as soon as*	Parts of the body **WordWise**: Expressions with *do when* and *if*
Unit 12 **Travel the world** p 110	Talking about travel and transport Talking about life experiences	Present perfect simple ▶ Present perfect with *ever* / *never* Present perfect vs. past simple	Transport and travel Travel verbs

Life Competencies: Dealing with negative feelings ▶, **Culture:** Hard journeys for schoolchildren ▶, Review

PRONUNCIATION	THINK!	SKILLS
/s/, /z/, /ɪz/ sounds	**Values:** Taking care of yourself	**Reading** Quiz: Do you enjoy life? Blog: What do you do in your free time? **Writing** Your routine **Listening** Conversations about hobbies
Contractions	**Values:** Fashion and clothes **Train to THINK:** Exploring numbers	**Reading** Chat conversation: Shopping Web forum: It's Sunday afternoon, what can I do? **Writing** An email to say what you're doing **Listening** Shop conversations

A2 Key for Schools Exam practice

Vowel sounds /ɪ/ and /iː/	**Values:** Food and health	**Reading** Online article: Creepy crawlies – the superfood of the future? Online blog: Eating around the world **Writing** A paragraph about what food you eat **Listening** In a café ordering food
-er /ə/ at the end of words	**Values:** Film families **Train to THINK:** Making inferences	**Reading** Blog: Old films, great families News article: Suzie saves her mum **Writing** An invitation **Listening** Why I love my family!

A2 Key for Schools Exam practice

-ed endings /d/, /t/, /ɪd/	**Values:** Following your dreams	**Reading** Magazine article: The 21st century caveman Holiday blog: Our holiday castle **Writing** A summary / a blog post **Listening** My favourite room
Stressed syllables in words	**Values:** Friendship **Train to THINK:** Making decisions	**Reading** Web article: A special friendship Magazine article: Life stories – Pen pals for years **Writing** A thank you note **Listening** Giving advice

A2 Key for Schools Exam practice

Vowel sounds: /ʊ/ and /uː/	**Values:** Caring for people and the environment	**Reading** Article: '… just because I didn't want to take a bath.' Website: Gadget reviews **Writing** A paragraph about housework **Listening** Radio programme: advice for young inventors
Strong and weak forms of *was* and *were*	**Values:** Trying, winning and losing **Train to THINK:** Sequencing	**Reading** Magazine article: The world's greatest sporting achievements Web forum: Sporting fails **Writing** An article about a sporting event **Listening** Teens talking about sport

A2 Key for Schools Exam practice

Vowel sounds: /ɪ/ and /aɪ/	**Values:** Valuing our world	**Reading** Magazine article: The wild side of life Blog: Extreme nature! **Writing** An email about an amazing weather event **Listening** Interview with a Kalahari bushman
Voiced /ð/ and unvoiced /θ/ consonants	**Values:** Appreciating other cultures **Train to THINK:** Problem solving	**Reading** Emails: Experiences in foreign countries Letters to a local government website: How can we improve our town? **Writing** An informal email **Listening** Teens making plans

A2 Key for Schools Exam practice

The /h/ consonant sound	**Values:** Exercise and health	**Reading** Magazine article: Changing bodies Blog: Old Wives' Tales **Writing** A phone message **Listening** Conversations about physical problems
Sentence stress	**Values:** Travel broadens the mind **Train to THINK:** Exploring differences	**Reading** Newspaper article: A world record breaker Magazine article: Travelling the world from your sofa! **Writing** An essay: Someone I admire **Listening** A traveller talking to a class

A2 Key for Schools Exam practice

Pronunciation pages 120–121   **Get it right!** pages 122–126   **Speaking activities** pages 127–128

WELCOME

A ALL ABOUT ME
Personal information

1 🔊 W.01 **Put the dialogue in order. Number the boxes. Listen and check.**

- [1] Ryan — Hi. I'm Ryan.
- [ ] Ryan — I'm thirteen. How about you?
- [ ] Ryan — Australia.
- [ ] Ryan — Hello, Claudia. Where are you from?
- [ ] Claudia — Me? I'm thirteen, too.
- [ ] Claudia — I'm from Brazil. And you?
- [ ] Claudia — Hi, Ryan. My name's Claudia.
- [ ] Claudia — Cool! How old are you, Ryan?

2 🔊 W.02 **Complete the dialogue with the phrases in the list. Listen and check.**

> are | meet | this | too

Ryan Claudia – ¹_____ is my friend Ahmed.
Ahmed Hi, Claudia. Nice to ²_____ you.
Claudia Nice to meet you, ³_____ , Ahmed. And this is my friend: her name's Laura.
Laura Hi, guys. How ⁴_____ you? I'm Laura. Laura Junqueira.

3 **SPEAKING** Imagine you are a famous person. Work in pairs, then in groups.
1 Tell your partner who you are.
2 Introduce your partner to the others in the group.

> Hi, I'm Tom Hardy.

> Hello, my name's Kate Middleton. And this is my friend Eden Hazard.

Nationalities and *be*

4 **Complete the names of the countries (add the consonants).**

1 _ e _ i _ o   7 _ _ a i _

2 _ u _ _ e _   8 _ _ a _ i _

3 I _ a _ _   9 _ o _ o _ _ i a

4 _ _ i _ a   10 A _ _ e _ _ i _ a

5 _ u _ _ i a   11 the U _ i _ e _ _ i _ _ _ o _

6 the U _ i _ e _ _ _ a _ e _   12 the _ e _ _ er _ a _ _ _

5 What nationality are the people? Write the sentences.

6 🔊 **W.03** Complete the dialogue with the correct forms of the verb *be*. Then listen and check.

Claudia So, Ahmed – where ⁰ _are_ you from?
Ahmed Me? I ¹____ from Britain. Ryan here ²____ from Australia, but I ³____ British.
Laura But ⁴____ your name British?
Ahmed Oh, good question. Well, no it ⁵____ . My parents ⁶____ from Egypt and so my name ⁷____ from Egypt, too. But my sister Fatima and I were both born here, so we ⁸____ 100% British.
Claudia That ⁹____ cool. I think your name ¹⁰____ really nice.
Ahmed Thank you! And you two, ¹¹____ you both Brazilian?
Laura That ¹²____ right. But we ¹³____ not from the same city. I ¹⁴____ from Belo Horizonte and Claudia ¹⁵____ from São Paulo. We ¹⁶____ students at the language school here.

Names and addresses

7 🔊 **W.04** Ahmed phones for a taxi. Listen and complete the information.

ABBEY'S TAXIS
Booking form
Taxi for ¹_____
Going to ²_____
Pick up at ³____ am/pm
From ⁴____ Street
Number of passengers ⁵____

8 🔊 **W.05** Now listen to a phone call. Correct each of these sentences.

0 Fernando phones Alejandra.
   No – Alejandra phones Fernando.
1 They met last Wednesday.
2 There's a party at Alejandra's place next Friday.
3 The party starts at seven thirty.
4 Alejandra lives at 134 Markam Avenue.
5 Her phone number is 0788 224 234.

B WHAT'S THAT?
Things in the classroom

1 Look at the pictures. Write the correct number next to each word.

board ☐ book ☐ CD ☐ chair ☐ desk ☐ floor ☐
pen ☐ pencil ☐ ruler ☐ window ☐ door ☐ notebook ☐

Prepositions of place

2 Look at the pictures. Choose the correct word.

0 The notebook is *under / (on) / behind* the chair.
1 The pencil is *on / in front of / under* the floor.
2 The pencil is *behind / between / under* the chair.
3 The book is *in / on / in front of* the desk.
4 The pen is *behind / under / in* the book.
5 The ruler is *in / between / under* the book.
6 The board is *in front of / between / behind* the door and the window.
7 The book is *under / on / in front of* the pen.

Classroom language

3 🔊 W.06 Complete each sentence with a word from the list. Listen and check.

> again | ask | don't | hand | me
> mean | page | say | spell | understand

1 Excuse _____ .
2 Can I _____ a question, please?
3 Can you say that _____ , please?
4 How do you _____ *comer* in English?
5 Open your books at _____ 56.
6 Put your _____ up if you know the answer.
7 Sorry, I _____ know.
8 Sorry, I don't _____ .
9 What does this word _____ ?
10 Excuse me. How do you _____ that word? Is it D-R-I-E-D or D-R-Y-E-D?

4 🔊 W.07 Use one of the sentences in Exercise 3 to complete each mini-dialogue. Listen and check.

1 Teacher Good morning, everyone.
  Student Good morning.
  Teacher OK. Let's start. _____
2 Teacher So, Michael, what's the answer?
  Michael _____
  Teacher That's OK. What about you, Susie?
3 Student _____ , Mrs McFarlane. I've got a question.
  Teacher Yes, what is it?
4 Student _____ : 'starving'?
  Teacher It means: 'very, very hungry'.

5 🔊 W.08 Put the dialogue in order. Number the boxes. Listen and check.

☐ A R-O-U-G-H.
☐ A No, that's completely wrong!
1 A How do you think you spell the word 'rough'?
☐ A No, that's really how you spell it.
☐ B OK, how do you spell it, then?
☐ B Oh. Let me think. Is it R-U-F?
☐ B You're kidding!

6 SPEAKING Work in pairs. Think of a word in English. Can your partner spell it?

How do you spell 'tomorrow'?

T-O-M-O-R-R-O-W.

That's right.

WELCOME

Object pronouns

7 Complete each sentence with the correct pronoun.

0 He's a good singer – we like <u>him</u> a lot.
1 My books are in your bag. Can you get _____ , please?
2 I've got a new bike – I'm going to ride _____ this afternoon.
3 Where are you? I can't see _____ .
4 I don't know where the Maths class is – can you show _____ ?
5 She doesn't know, so please tell _____ .
6 We like our parents. They give _____ lots of love!

this / that / these / those

8 Match the pictures and sentences.

1 What animal is this?
2 What animal is that?
3 These shoes are nice.
4 Those shoes are nice.

9 Complete the email by writing the words in the correct spaces. There are three extra words.

<del>are</del> | do | does | how | it | lot | me | them | there | understand | what | who

Liz
lima565@email.co.uk

Hello from Italy

Hi Liz,
I'm writing to you from Italy! My family and I ⁰ <u>are</u> on holiday here for a week. It's really nice here. Italian people are very friendly, but of course I don't speak Italian, so I don't ¹_____ when people talk to me. But a ²_____ of people here speak English, so it's all OK.

Our hotel is great. ³_____ is a gym downstairs with a swimming pool – it's really big! I have dinner late – usually after eight o'clock! And it's always really good – the pasta is delicious, but I usually have pizza. Dinner is my favourite meal – I love ⁴_____ .

So, ⁵_____ are you? I hope you are enjoying your holiday, too. I want to buy a present for you here in Italy. ⁶_____ would you like? ⁷_____ you like Italian music? Write and tell ⁸_____ , OK?

Have a good time and write soon.
Love,
James

A

C

B

D

7

C ABOUT TIME
Days and dates

1 🔊 **W.09** Listen and choose the correct information.

Nathan Hi, Kim. Why are you so happy today?
Kim Because it's the ¹21st / 22nd / 23rd of February.
Nathan And what's special about that date?
Kim It's my birthday!
Nathan Really! Happy birthday, Kim.
Kim Thanks. I'm ²12 / 13 / 14 today.
Nathan Lucky you!
Kim When is your birthday, Nathan?
Nathan It's in ³August / September / October.
Kim What date?
Nathan The ⁴11th / 12th / 13th. I think it's on a ⁵Tuesday / Thursday / Friday this year.

2 🔊 **W.10** Complete the names of the days and months. Listen and check.

DAYS
1 M _o n d a y_
2 T _ _ s d _ _
3 W _ _ n _ _ d _ _
4 _ h u _ _ _ _ _ y
5 F _ _ _ _ _ _ _
6 S _ _ _ _ r _ _ _ _
7 S _ _ _ _ _ _ _

MONTHS
1 J _ _ _ u _ _ y
2 F _ b r u _ _ _ _
3 M _ _ _ _ h
4 _ p _ _ l
5 M _ _
6 J _ _ _ _
7 J _ _ y
8 A _ _ u _ _
9 S _ _ _ _ _ m b e r
10 O _ _ _ _ _ _ e r
11 _ _ v e m _ _ _ _
12 D _ _ _ _ _ _ _ _

3 Match the numbers and the words.

first	15th
second	12th
third	22nd
fourth	20th
fifth	31st
twelfth	3rd
fifteenth	1st
twentieth	2nd
twenty-second	4th
thirty-first	5th

4 🔊 **W.11** How do you say these numbers? Listen and check.

6th | 12th | 16th | 19th | 22nd | 23rd | 30th

5 🔊 **W.12** Listen and write the people's birthdays.

1 _____15th June_____

4 _____

2 _____

5 _____

3 _____

6 _____

6 **SPEAKING** Walk around the classroom. Ask and answer questions. Whose birthday is close to your birthday?

When's your birthday? *It's on 17th March.*

My day

7 Put the photos in the order you do them.

A ☐ I do my homework.

E ☐ I have breakfast.

B ☐ I get home.

F ☐ I go to bed.

C ☐ I get up.

G ☐ I have dinner.

D ☐ I have lunch.

H ☐ I go to school.

8 Look at the sentences in Exercise 7. Write them in the correct column <u>for you</u>.

Morning	Afternoon	Evening
I get up.		

9 Match the clocks and the times.
1 It's ten to one.
2 It's six o'clock.
3 It's half past three.
4 It's eight o'clock.
5 It's ten to eight.
6 It's 10.30.
7 It's twenty past ten.
8 It's half past eight.

A **3**
I _get home._

B ☐
I _____

E ☐
I _____

C ☐
I _____

F ☐
I _____

D ☐
I _____

G ☐
I _____

H ☐
I _____

10 🔊 W.13 Listen to Mayra. Write about her day under the pictures in Exercise 9.

> **Look** 👁
> midday to midnight = pm   midnight to midday = am
> 12 am = midnight   12 pm = midday
> 1 am = 1 o'clock in the morning
> 1 pm = 1 o'clock in the afternoon

11 SPEAKING Work in pairs. Talk about your day.

I go to school at half past eight.

I do my homework at seven o'clock.

D MY THINGS
My possessions

1 Read Jack's blog and tick (✓) the photos of the things he has got.

2 Work in pairs. Put the things Jack mentions in his blog in the correct list.

PERSONAL POSSESSIONS: _TV_ , _laptop_ , _____ , _____ , _____ , _____

PETS: _cat_ , _____

Welcome!
Hi, my name's Jack.
I've got a phone – it's really my favourite thing!
I haven't got a pet, but I'd love a cat or maybe something unusual like a lizard.
I haven't got a laptop. I want one for my next birthday.
I've got a bike and I've got a skateboard.
I haven't got a scooter. My dad's got an electric one and I sometimes use that.
I haven't got a TV in my bedroom, but there is one in the living room and the kitchen.
I'm very lucky!

have got

3 Complete the table with *'ve*, *'s*, *have*, *has*, *haven't* or *hasn't*.

Positive	Negative
I've (have) got a pet.	I haven't (have not) got a dog.
You ¹_____ (have) got a pet.	You ⁵_____ (have not) got a dog.
He's (has) got a pet.	He hasn't (has not) got a dog.
She ²_____ (has) got a pet.	She ⁶_____ (has not) got a dog.
We ³_____ (have) got a pet.	We ⁷_____ (have not) got a dog.
They ⁴_____ (have) got a pet.	They ⁸_____ (have not) got a dog.

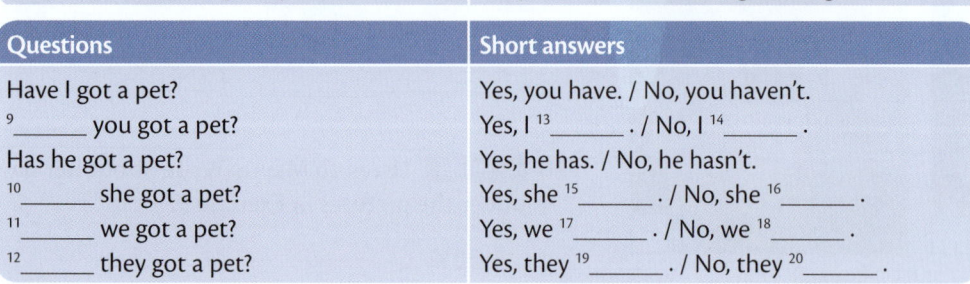

Questions	Short answers
Have I got a pet?	Yes, you have. / No, you haven't.
⁹_____ you got a pet?	Yes, I ¹³_____ . / No, I ¹⁴_____ .
Has he got a pet?	Yes, he has. / No, he hasn't.
¹⁰_____ she got a pet?	Yes, she ¹⁵_____ . / No, she ¹⁶_____ .
¹¹_____ we got a pet?	Yes, we ¹⁷_____ . / No, we ¹⁸_____ .
¹²_____ they got a pet?	Yes, they ¹⁹_____ . / No, they ²⁰_____ .

4 Complete the sentences with *have*, *has*, *haven't* or *hasn't* so they are true for you.

1 I _____ got a tablet.
2 My mum _____ got a computer.
3 I _____ got a cat.
4 My best friend _____ got a sister.
5 I _____ got a computer in my bedroom.
6 My family _____ got two cars.

5 **SPEAKING** Walk around the classroom. Find someone who has got …

1 a blue bike
2 a cat
3 a lot of books
4 a TV in his/her bedroom
5 two brothers or sisters
6 a laptop
7 an unusual pet
8 a house with a garden

Have you got a bike? *Yes, I have.* *What colour is it?*

I like and *I'd like*

6 Match the pictures and the sentences.

A

C

B

D

1 I like oranges.
2 I'd like an orange.
3 I like showers.
4 I'd like a shower.

7 W.14 Complete with *I like* or *I'd like*. Listen and check.

0 A What's your favourite food?
  B _I like_ pizza best.
1 A Can I help you?
  B Yes, _____ a hot dog.
2 A _____ an ice cream, please.
  B Chocolate or strawberry?
3 A What do you want to watch?
  B Well, _____ comedies, so can we watch something funny, please?
4 A _____ football. Do you?
  B Not much. I think tennis is better.
5 A Do you want a pet for your birthday?
  B _____ a cat, please!

8 Complete with the words in the list.

apple juice | chicken | ice cream | orange

Lunch Box

Sandwiches:
cheese or 1_____

Desserts:
cake or 2_____

Fruit:
apple or 3_____

Drinks:
water or 4_____

9 W.15 Listen to the dialogue. What does Oscar choose for his lunch?

10 W.15 Write the questions to complete part of the dialogue. Listen again and check.

What fruit would you like?
Have you got oranges?
What would you like for lunch today?
Would you like a chicken sandwich or a cheese sandwich?

A Hi, Oscar.
  1 _____
B I'd like a lunch box, please.
A 2 _____
B A chicken sandwich, please.
A 3 _____
B 4 _____
A Yes, we have.
B An orange, please.

11 SPEAKING Work in pairs. Make a picnic box for your partner. Ask and answer questions.

What would you like for ... ?

Would you like a ... or ... ?

1 HAVING A GOOD TIME

OBJECTIVES

FUNCTIONS: talking about routines and everyday activities; expressing likes and dislikes; giving warnings and stating prohibition; talking about free time activities

GRAMMAR: present simple review; like + -ing; adverbs of frequency

VOCABULARY: hobbies; collocations with *have*

Get TH!NKING

Watch the video and think: what makes you happy?

 A
 B
 C
 D
 E
 F
 G
 H

READING

1 **Match the activities and the photos.**
   1 sleeping
   2 doing homework
   3 doing exercise
   4 messaging on your phone
   5 reading
   6 dancing
   7 doing housework
   8 singing

2 **Do you enjoy these activities? Write *always*, *sometimes* or *never*.**
   1 Sleeping is _____ fun.
   2 Reading is _____ boring.
   3 Doing homework is _____ interesting.
   4 Dancing is _____ easy.
   5 Doing exercise is _____ boring.
   6 Doing housework is _____ difficult.
   7 Messaging on my phone is _____ fun.
   8 Singing is _____ difficult.

3 **SPEAKING** Work in groups of three and compare your ideas from Exercise 2.

I think reading is sometimes boring.

Really? I think it's never boring.

4 **SPEAKING** Think of more activities and say what you think.

Playing football is always fun.

Studying is sometimes interesting.

5 🔊 **1.01** Read and listen to the quiz on page 13. Then take the quiz and compare your score with a partner.

12

Do you ENJOY LIFE?

HAVING A GOOD TIME — UNIT 1

Do your parents always ask you to do housework? Does your teacher give you homework every day? Life is sometimes difficult because there are lots of things to do. It's great to be busy, but it's important to look after yourself and have fun, too. We all need to think about ourselves and do things we like, whether it is playing an instrument or taking photos. But we also need to do things that keep us healthy and happy.

Here's our quiz. Try it and find out: do you have lots of fun?

1 Do you laugh a lot?
A Yes, I laugh all the time.
B I only laugh when I'm happy.
C My best friend says I don't laugh very often.

2 How many hobbies do you have?
A I have lots of hobbies.
B one
C I don't have any hobbies.

3 When do you listen to music?
A in the morning, afternoon and evening
B I only listen to music when I have time.
C I never listen to music. I don't have time.

4 How many hours do you sleep a night?
A 9–10 hours
B about 8 hours
C less than 8 hours

5 Do you like doing exercise?
A Yes, exercise is fun.
B Some exercise is OK, but not everything.
C I don't like exercise at all.

6 Do you like word and number puzzles?
A I like puzzles a lot.
B Word puzzles are OK, but number puzzles are boring.
C No, I don't like puzzles at all.

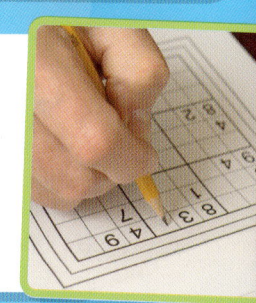

7 Which of these activities do you do most?
A spend time with friends and family
B message friends online or on my phone
C watch TV or play games on my phone

YOUR SCORE:
Mostly As: Wow! You know how to have fun and enjoy life.
Mostly Bs: Hmm, OK, but can you do more? Try and find more time for yourself.
Mostly Cs: Try and find more ways to have more fun.

TH!NK values
Taking care of yourself

6 Which questions in the quiz tell us that these things are important for us?

a [7] Being with people
b [ ] Enjoying exercise
c [ ] Sleep
d [ ] Enjoying music
e [ ] Giving your brain exercise
f [ ] Being positive
g [ ] Having interests

7 SPEAKING Compare your ideas with a partner.

Question 7 shows us that being with people is important.

13

GRAMMAR
Present simple review

1 **Complete the sentences with the words in the list. Check your answers in the quiz on page 13.**

> do | does | don't | ~~like~~ | says

0 I _like_ puzzles a lot.
1 My best friend _____ I don't laugh very often.
2 I _____ like exercise at all.
3 _____ your teacher give you homework every day?
4 _____ you like doing exercise?

2 **Look at the sentences in Exercise 1 and the table. Complete the rule with *do*, *does*, *don't* or *doesn't*.**

Positive	Negative
I **like** films.	I **don't like** films.
You **like** films.	You **don't like** films.
He/She/It **likes** films.	He/She/It **doesn't like** films.
We **like** films.	We **don't like** films.
They **like** films.	They **don't like** films.

Questions	Short answers	
Do I **like** films?	Yes, you **do**.	No, you **don't**.
Do you **like** films?	Yes, I **do**.	No, I **don't**.
Does he/she/it **like** films?	Yes, he/she/it **does**.	No, he/she/it **doesn't**.
Do we **like** films?	Yes, we **do**.	No, we **don't**.
Do they **like** films?	Yes, they **do**.	No, they **don't**.

RULE: Use the present simple for things that happen regularly or that are always true.
In positive sentences:
- with *I*, *you*, *we* and *they*, use the base form of the verb.
- with *he*, *she* and *it*, add *-s* (or *-es* with verbs that end in *-s*, *-sh*, *-ch*, *-x* or *-z*).

In negative sentences:
- with *I*, *you*, *we* and *they*, use ¹_____ .
- with *he*, *she* and *it*, use ²_____ .

In questions:
- with *I*, *you*, *we* and *they*, use the auxiliary ³_____ .
- with *he*, *she* and *it*, use the auxiliary ⁴_____ .

3 **Complete the sentences. Use the present simple form of the verbs.**

0 I _don't like_ (not like) horror movies.
  I _get_ (get) really scared watching them.
1 My dad _____ (not sleep) a lot.
  He only _____ (need) five or six hours.
2 A _____ you _____ (study) English?
  B Yes, I _____ .
3 My brother _____ (cook) really well, but he says he _____ (not enjoy) it.
4 A _____ your sister _____ (play) in the school football team?
  B No, she _____ .
5 My grandparents _____ (not like) travelling.
  They _____ (prefer) to stay at home.
6 My best friend _____ (watch) TV all day.
  He _____ (not do) anything else.

→ workbook page 10

PRONUNCIATION
/s/, /z/, /ɪz/ sounds Go to page 120.

VOCABULARY
Hobbies

4 **Complete the phrases with the words in the list.**

> be | collect | keep | ~~play~~ | take | write

0 to _play_ an instrument   3 to _____ photos
1 to _____ in a club   4 to _____ a pet
2 to _____ a blog   5 to _____ things

5 **SPEAKING** Work in pairs. Ask questions about the hobbies in the photos.

Do you play an instrument?
What do you play?
Do you collect something? What ...?

→ workbook page 12

HAVING A GOOD TIME UNIT 1

🎧 LISTENING

6 🔊 1.04 Listen to the conversations. Which one goes with each picture? Write 1–3 in the boxes.

 A
 B
 C

7 🔊 1.04 Listen again. Complete the sentences with the names in the list.

| Jade | Harry | Harry's mum | Ben | ~~Sally~~ | Dad's friend |

0 _____Sally_____ has Geography homework to do.
1 _____ loves his hobby.
2 _____ wants to do judo lessons.
3 _____ thinks judo is good for strength.
4 _____ thinks puzzles are good for the brain.
5 _____ doesn't like crosswords.

WordWise: Collocations with *have*

8 Match the sentence halves.

1 ☐ How many hobbies
2 ☐ I only listen to music
3 ☐ You know how to *have fun*
4 ☐ I'm hungry.
5 ☐ It's my hobby
6 ☐ Why don't you *have a rest*

a when I *have time*.
b and stop playing for a while?
c *Let's have dinner.*
d and enjoy life.
e *do you have*?
f and I *have a good time* when I practise.

→ workbook page 12

9 Copy the diagram into your notebook and complete it with the hobbies in the list.

| playing the piano | joining a tennis club
| collecting stamps | writing a blog
| dancing | cooking | watching TV
| playing online games | taking photos

Make friends

playing the piano

Relax   *Discover your talents*

10 SPEAKING Ask and answer the questions in pairs.

1 Who do you have the most fun with?
2 Do you have a good time at school?
3 How many hobbies have you got?
4 What time do you have dinner?
5 Do you have a rest after school?
6 Do you always have time to do your homework?

READING

1 🔊 1.05 Read and listen to the text about collecting things.

What do you do in your FREE TIME?

OK, we know you all like watching TV and playing computer games, but we want to know some of the other things you do when you've got some free time. Write and let us know.

I love cats! I like watching cat videos on YouTube every day. I love taking photos of them, too, cats that I see when I'm outside – I try to get photos of lots of different kinds. And I collect things with cats on them – you know, cards or notebooks or T-shirts, things like that. But we can't have cats at home because my dad can't stand them!
Hermione 👍6 💬2

I can't stand having nothing to do – for example, when I wait for the bus or in the queue at the fast food place – so I always have my puzzle app on my mobile. Sometimes it's Sudoku, sometimes a crossword or different word game, but it doesn't matter – I just love doing puzzles. And it's great because I never get bored.
Andy 👍9 💬1

I'm usually busy, but occasionally I've got a bit of free time, especially in the evening after I do my homework. My favourite thing is looking at maps online. I like using 'street view' and I imagine myself walking in a street somewhere. My dream is to go to New York, so I often 'walk' in the streets there. I try and visit a different place in the world at least once a week.
Natalie 👍4 💬0

I don't really like sport – I hate running and doing exercise and all that – but I'm crazy about the New Zealand rugby team, the All Blacks. It's because my uncle and aunt live there and they love rugby, so I watch the games and collect anything I can about them! I have a book that I put photos and newspaper articles in. Once a week my uncle and I talk on the internet about the All Blacks – I love that!
Lucy 👍1 💬6

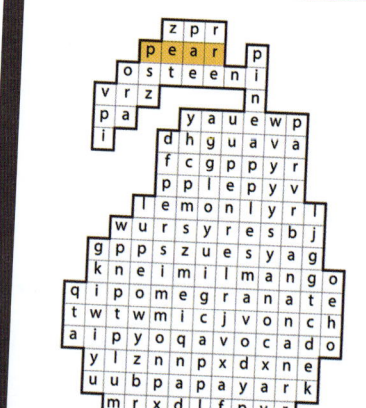

2 Read the sentences. Which of the people above do you think is saying each one?

0 I've got a great bag with a picture of a cat on it. — **Hermione**

1 My favourite player is called Beauden Barrett. _____

2 The Empire State Building is on Fifth Avenue. _____

3 I love walking around in Rome, too. _____

4 There are some really good ones in my dad's newspaper. _____

5 I love the ones with long hair – they're called Persian. _____

HAVING A GOOD TIME   UNIT 1

GRAMMAR
like + -ing

3 Look at the sentences from the blog on page 16. Draw 😊 or ☹️ next to each one.
1 I just love <u>doing</u> puzzles. _____
2 I can't stand <u>having</u> nothing to do. _____
3 I hate <u>running</u>. _____
4 I like <u>using</u> 'street view'. _____

4 Use the sentences in Exercise 3 to complete the rule.

> **RULE:** Use the ¹_____ form of the verb after verbs which express likes and dislikes,
> e.g., **like, love, hate, enjoy, can't stand.**
> • To make this form, add ²_____ to the base verb.
> • If the verb ends in -e, drop the final -e (e.g., *live – living*).
> • If a short verb ends in a consonant + vowel + consonant, we usually double the final consonant before adding the -ing (e.g., *swim – swimming*).

5 Complete the sentences. Use the *-ing* form of the verbs in the list.

| eat | ride | ~~run~~ | swim | talk | visit |

0 I hate ___running___ to catch the bus to school.
1 My parents enjoy _____ in different places.
2 My brother can't stand _____ on the phone.
3 They like _____ in the sea when it's warm.
4 Donna really likes _____ her bike.
5 We love _____ new places on holiday.

6 [WRITING] What about you? Write two or three sentences about what you like doing. Use the ideas in Exercises 3 and 5 to help you.

→ workbook page 11

Adverbs of frequency

7 Complete the diagram with the words in the list.

| always | never | occasionally | often |

8 Complete the sentences so they are true for you.
1 I _____ do my homework when I get home.
2 I _____ write 'thank you' cards for my presents.
3 I am _____ late for school.
4 I _____ watch TV in the mornings.
5 Mum is _____ angry if I don't tidy my room.
6 I _____ turn off the lights when I leave the room.

9 Complete these sentences from the blog on page 16. Check your answers and complete the rule.
1 I like watching cat videos on YouTube _____ _____ .
2 _____ _____ _____ my uncle and I talk on the internet.

> **RULE:** Words like *sometimes, never, always* come ³*before / after* the verb *be* but ⁴*before / after* other verbs. Phrases like *every day* or *twice a week* can come at the beginning or at the end of a sentence.

10 Write down things you do …
every day: <u>I text my best friend every day.</u>
three times a week: _____
once a year: _____

11 [SPEAKING] Work in small groups. Compare your answers to Exercises 8 and 10.

How often do you go to the cinema? *I go once a month …*

→ workbook page 11

WRITING
Your routine

12 Complete the sentences so they are true for you.
1 I rarely _____ at the weekend.
2 I can't stand _____ .
3 I _____ three times every day.
4 I love _____ in August.
5 I never _____ when I'm tired.
6 I _____ once a week.
7 I occasionally _____ .
8 I enjoy _____ after school.

Adverbs of frequency

0%   rarely   sometimes   usually   100%

1 _____ 2 _____ 3 _____ 4 _____

17

DEVELOPING SPEAKING

1 🔊 **1.06** Look at the photo. What do you think it is? How do you know? Read and listen to check.

Zoey: So, have you got any hobbies at all, Ellie?
Ellie: Yes, actually. I really enjoy making model aeroplanes.
Zoey: Model aeroplanes? That sounds cool.
Ellie: It is. Do you want to see them?
Zoey: Yes, please!!
Ellie: OK. Come on. They're upstairs in my bedroom.
moments later ...
Ellie: And here are my planes. That's my favourite.
Zoey: Cool! Can I pick it up?
Ellie: OK, but be careful. No, please! Don't do that! They don't fly!
Zoey: Oh, that's right. OK. Sorry.
Mum: Ellie? What are you up to?
Ellie: Nothing, Mum. My friend Zoey's here. We're looking at my planes.
Mum: OK. But hurry up! Dinner's almost ready.
Ellie: OK, Mum. Look out, Zoey! It's very …
Zoey: Oh no. It's broken!
Ellie: Yes, I know!
Zoey: I'm really sorry, Ellie. And it's your favourite, too.
Ellie: That's OK. I know it's an accident. I'm sure I can fix it.

2 Read the dialogue again and answer the questions.
 1 Where are Ellie's planes?
 2 What do Ellie's planes not do?
 3 Why does Ellie's mum ask her to hurry up?
 4 What does Zoey do to the plane?

3 **SPEAKING** Discuss the questions in pairs.
 1 Is Zoey really upset?
 2 What should she do?
 3 How does Ellie really feel?

Phrases for fluency

4 Find expressions (1–5) in the dialogue. Who says them? Match them to the definitions (a–f).

 0 (What are you) up to?   *Mum*   e
 1 Cool! _____ ☐
 2 Come on. _____ ☐
 3 That's right. _____ ☐
 4 Hurry up. _____ ☐
 5 Look out! _____ ☐

 a Be quick.   b Be careful.   c Let's go.
 d Correct.   e Doing.   f Great.

5 Complete the conversation with the expressions in Exercise 4.

 Sarah Hi, Nicole. What are you ⁰_____ up to _____?
 Nicole Oh, just walking. Are you here for a walk, too?
 Sarah ¹_____ . I'm a bit bored at home.
 Nicole Me, too. We can walk together, if you want.
 Sarah ²_____ ! Oh no – ³_____ ! Mike Smith is coming. I don't like him!
 Nicole ⁴_____ . Let's walk over here.
 Sarah I don't want him to see me. ⁵_____ , Nicole!

FUNCTIONS
Giving warnings and stating prohibition

KEY LANGUAGE
1 **Be careful**, Nora.
2 **Look out**, Geoff.
3 **Don't do** that.
4 **Don't talk** in here!

6 Match the sentences from the Key Language box with the pictures A–D.

A

C

B

D

7 Complete the mini-dialogues with the expressions from the Key Language box.

 1 **David** The baby is asleep.
   Liam I know. _____
 2 **Olivia** Let's cross the road here.
   Julia Wait! _____ There's a car coming.

8 **WRITING** In pairs write short dialogues for the other two expressions.

HAVING A GOOD TIME · UNIT 1

LIFE COMPETENCIES

Empathy is being able to understand and share other people's feelings. We need empathy to tell people we understand how they feel in bad situations. Sometimes, this is all people need when they feel bad. But empathy can help us decide what we can do to help.

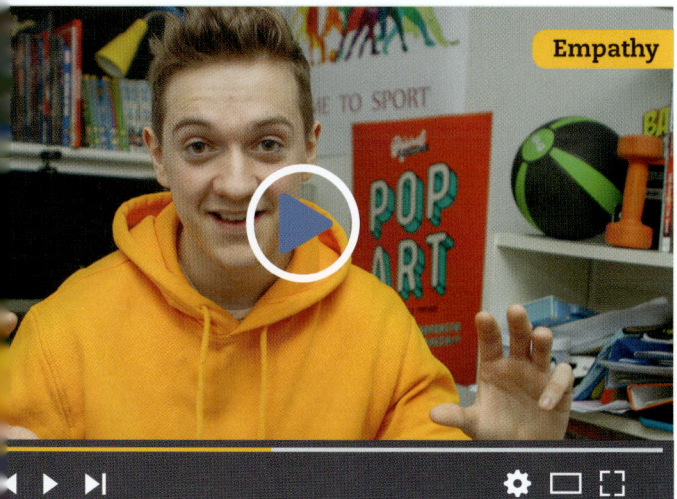

Empathy

1 ▶ 03 **Watch the video. How many detentions does the vlogger get?**

2 ▶ 03 **Watch and write K (Kate) or M (Mum) to complete the sentences.**

1 ☐ just says 'whatever'.
2 ☐ wants to know about his day.
3 ☐ doesn't have empathy.
4 ☐ has empathy.
5 ☐ cares how he feels.
6 ☐ doesn't care at all.

3 ▶ 03 **Watch again and match the person (a–d) with the problem (1–4). What can you say to each person to show you care?**

1 ☐ My back hurts.   a Dad
2 ☐ I don't like my boss. b Vlogger
3 ☐ I need a holiday.   c Mum
4 ☐ I'm having a bad day. d Teacher

TIPS FOR SHOWING EMPATHY

- Listen to other people's problems. Don't always talk about your problems.
- When someone is explaining their problems, don't say their problems aren't important or be critical.
- It's not always necessary to give advice. Sometimes just listening and understanding is enough.

4 **Read the email from Jack to his friend Manny. Does he like his new school?**

 Jack
Jack023@thinkmail.com

Hey!

Hi Manny,

How are you? Thanks for your email and the photos! I like the holiday pictures, but my favourite is the class photo. Say 'Hi' to everyone for me! Who is the new girl next to you in the photo?

I don't like my new school very much. The teachers are mostly OK, but I can't stand going to Maths now. Mr Allen, the teacher, always seems angry because I don't know things that the rest of the class know from last year. I don't think I can pass the exam we have next week because I don't ask questions anymore.

Another thing is that I haven't got any friends. Everyone has got a small group of friends and isn't interested in talking to me – 'the new boy'. Luckily, I have a new mobile, so I can spend break playing games, but it's horrible when nobody wants to sit next to me in class, and the teacher moves someone to be my partner.

Are you free to Skype this weekend? Let me know, OK?

Jack

5 SPEAKING **Work in pairs. Discuss the questions about Jack.**

1 What are Jack's problems at his new school?
2 Imagine you are Jack. How do you feel?
3 When do your friends and family feel like this?
4 Do people like talking about these feelings?

6 **Imagine you are Manny. Which of these sentences are good to say to Jack?**

- I'm here for you.
- I've got some great friends!
- I'm sorry you feel this way.
- Talking about feelings is silly.
- I understand how you feel.

Me and my world

7 SPEAKING **Write names to complete the list. Discuss with a partner.**

a The people who care most about me are …
b The people I care most about are …
c The people I want to care more about are …

8 **Give examples of how you give and receive empathy from the people in Exercise 7.**

'When my mum is unhappy, I give her a hug.'

19

2 SPENDING MONEY

Get TH!NKING
Watch the video and think: why do people shop?

OBJECTIVES

FUNCTIONS:
buying clothes in a shop; talking about what people are doing at the moment

GRAMMAR:
present continuous; verbs of perception; present simple vs. present continuous

VOCABULARY:
shops; clothes

1 €2.50

2 £24.65

3 $299

4 £3.99

5 $0.50

6 £599

READING

1 🔊 2.01 Say the prices. Listen and check.

2 🔊 2.02 Match the objects with the prices in Exercise 1. Write 1–6 in the boxes. Listen and check.

 A ☐

 D ☐

 B ☐ E ☐

 C ☐ F ☐

3 **SPEAKING** Work in pairs. Discuss the questions. Then compare your ideas with other students.

Which of the things in Exercise 2 do you …
1 think are cheap?
2 think are expensive?
3 think are fantastic?
4 dream about having?

4 Look at the photos on page 21. What clothes can you see?

5 🔊 2.03 Read and listen to Mike and Hannah's messages. How much are each of the clothes in the photos?

6 Mark the sentences T (true) or F (false). Correct the false ones.

0 Hannah is at a friend's house watching TV.
   Hannah is at home watching TV.
1 Mike is in a shop in Green Street.
   _____
2 Barker's is a big chemist's in Market Street.
   _____
3 Mike needs ten minutes to arrive at Barker's.
   _____
4 There are lots of people in Barker's.
   _____
5 Hannah doesn't want to join Mike because she's busy.
   _____

 # Messages SPENDING MONEY UNIT 2

 **Hannah** ● Online Photo Call  Video

Mike: Hi, Hannah. What are you up to?

 **Hannah:** Hey, Mike. Nothing much. I'm at home. I'm watching some TV, but it's not very good. I don't want to do my homework! How about you?

Mike: I'm in town. Shopping. I'm looking for a new jacket. Do you like this one? It's £20.

 **Hannah:** Erm. It's OK. It looks a bit old-fashioned though. Which shop are you in? Tell me you're not looking for clothes in that old place in Green Street.

Mike: Hah! Of course I am! You know I always like to buy my clothes here.

 **Hannah:** But their clothes are all second-hand. And that means they're old-fashioned.

Mike: I like the clothes here – they're really cool and they're cheap. I'm not rich like you, you know!

 **Hannah:** Me? Rich? You're joking of course. Hahaha. Go to Barker's next to the big chemist's in Market Street. They've got a sale on. They're selling everything at 30% off the original price! And their stuff's really nice. I'm wearing one of their T-shirts now. Only £9.99!

Mike: Yeah, that's cool. And 30% off? Brilliant. OK, I'm going there now. Oh no! Now it's raining and I haven't got an umbrella. OK, it's not far. Five minutes and I'm there.

Mike: OK, here I am in Barker's. The shop's really crowded. It's because of the sale, I guess.

 Hannah: Maybe my mum's there. She's doing some shopping at the moment. So … anything nice?

Mike: Yeah! Look at this shirt! Only £25! I want it!

 **Hannah:** Mike, are you crazy? It's awful.

Mike: No, it's not. I love wearing bright colours. They make me feel happy. It's perfect for a rainy day.

 **Hannah:** I think you're wasting your money and my time. Anyway – are you looking for a jacket or a shirt?

Mike: Oh yes, you're right. You're better at clothes than me. Come and help me. You're not doing anything, are you?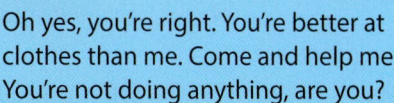

 Hannah: That sounds like a bad idea. It's raining – remember?

TH!NK values

Fashion and clothes

7 **How important are these for you? Give each one a number from 0 to 5 (0 = not important, 5 = very, very important).**

Clothes – my values:
- [ ] I want to look cool.
- [ ] I want to feel comfortable.
- [ ] I always buy cheap clothes.
- [ ] I like buying designer clothes.
- [ ] I love wearing clean clothes.
- [ ] I like wearing bright colours.
- [ ] I always buy clothes in the same shops.

8 **SPEAKING Work in pairs. Ask and answer questions.**

How important is it for you to look cool?

Not very important. I have 3 points. What about you?

For me, it's very important. 5 points.

21

GRAMMAR
Present continuous

1 **Look at the examples of the present continuous in the chat on page 21. Who says these lines? Mark them (M) Mike or (H) Hannah in the boxes.**

   1 I'm **looking** for a new jacket. ☐
   2 Now it's **raining**. ☐
   3 She's **doing** some shopping at the moment. ☐
   4 **Are** you **looking** for a jacket or a shirt? ☐

2 **Complete the rule and the table.**

> **RULE:** Use the present ¹_____ to talk about things that are happening at or around the time of speaking. Form the present continuous with the present simple of ²_____ + the *-ing* form (e.g., *running / doing / wearing*, etc.) of the main verb.

Positive	Negative
I'm (= I am) working.	I'm not working.
You/we/they're (³_____) working.	You/we/they aren't working.
He/she/it's (is) working.	He/she/it ⁴_____ working.

Questions	Short answers
⁵_____ I working?	Yes, I am. / No, I'm not.
⁶_____ you/we/they working?	Yes, you/we/they ⁸_____ . No, you/we/they ⁹_____ .
⁷_____ he/she/it working?	Yes, he/she/it ¹⁰_____ . No, he/she/it ¹¹_____ .

3 **Complete the sentences. Use the present continuous form of the verbs.**

   0 Sorry, Jenny's not here. *She's doing* some shopping in town.
   1 They're in the living room.
      They _____ (play) computer games.
   2 Henry's in the garage.
      He _____ (clean) his bike.
   3 Steven! You _____ (not listen) to me!
   4 I can't talk now. I _____ (do) my homework.
   5 It's 3-0! We _____ (not play) very well, and we _____ (lose)!
   6 A _____ you _____ (watch) this programme?
      B No, I _____ . You can watch a different one if you want.
   7 A What _____ Anna _____ (do)?
      B She _____ (not tidy) her room.
      She _____ (play) video games!

→ workbook page 18

VOCABULARY
Shops

4 **Write the names of the shops under the photos.**

> bookshop | chemist's | clothes shop
> coffee shop | department store
> mobile phone shop | sports shop | supermarket

1 _____

5 _____

2 _____

6 _____

3 _____

7 _____

4 _____

8 _____

5 **SPEAKING Complete the sentences with the names of shops from Exercise 4. Then compare your ideas with other students.**

   1 In my town there's a very good …
      It's called … It's good because …
   2 I often go there because …
   3 I never go into … because they don't interest me.
      I don't often go to … because …

> *In my town there's a very good clothes shop. It's good because the clothes aren't expensive.*

→ workbook page 20

SPENDING MONEY   UNIT 2

GRAMMAR
Verbs of perception

6 Look at the sentences from the text on page 21. Answer the questions.

1 *It looks a bit old-fashioned though.* What is 'it'?
2 *That sounds like a bad idea.* What is 'that'?

7 Match the verbs with the pictures. Then complete the rule.

1 look   2 sound   3 smell   4 taste

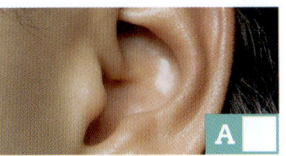
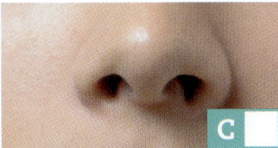
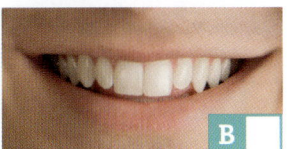
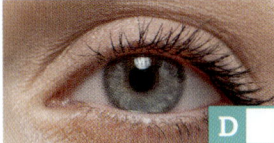

RULE: Verbs of perception are used in the present ⁵*simple / continuous* when they are used to give an opinion.
*The food **tastes** great.*   *That idea **sounds** good.*
*That pizza **smells** nice.*   *His new shirt **looks** awful!*
The words after the verbs of perception are ⁶*nouns / adjectives*.

8 Match the responses (a–d) to the first parts of the conversations (1–4).

1 I'm going to the park. ☐
2 My mother's making bread. ☐
3 I'm wearing my new clothes. ☐
4 Don't you like the juice? ☐

a No. It tastes horrible!   c It smells fantastic.
b That sounds great.   d They look nice.

→ workbook page 19

LISTENING

9 🔊 2.04 Listen. What shop is each person in? Write 1–4. Two shops are not used.

☐ bookshop   ☐ chemist's
☐ clothes shop   ☐ sports shop
☐ supermarket   ☐ mobile phone shop

10 🔊 2.04 Listen again. What is each person buying?

FUNCTIONS
Buying things in a shop

11 Read the sentences. Mark them C (customer) or A (assistant).

0 Can I help you?   A
1 Have you got … ?   __
2 What size do you take?   __
3 Can I try it/them on, please?   __
4 How much is it/are they?   __
5 That's (twenty pounds), please.   __
6 Have you got it/them in (blue)?   __
7 Can I pay with my contactless card?   __
8 I can't find the price.   __
9 Would you like the receipt?   __

12 Complete the dialogue with the missing words.

A Hello. Can I ¹_____ you?
B Yes, please. I like these shoes. Have you ²_____ them in black?
A Yes, we ³_____ .
B Great. Can I ⁴_____ them on?
A Yes, of course. What size do you ⁵_____ ?
B I'm a ⁶_____ 42 … They're very nice. I'll take them. How ⁷_____ are they?
A They're £75.
B I don't have cash. Can I pay with my ⁸_____ ?
A Yes, of course.

ROLE PLAY Buying things in a shop

Work in pairs. Student A: Go to page 127.
Student B: Go to page 128. Take two or three minutes to prepare. Then have two conversations.

Train to TH!NK

Exploring numbers

13 You want to buy some new clothes. Here are some things you like. Answer the questions in pairs.

T-shirt – £10.50   shoes – £35.75   jumper – £18.25
belt – £6.50   jacket – £55

1 Choose three things. How much do they cost?
2 You've got £40. Name three things you can buy.
3 You've got £85. Can you buy all five things?

14 SPEAKING Compare your ideas with a partner.

PRONUNCIATION
Contractions Go to page 120. 🎧

VOCABULARY
Clothes

1 🔊 2.07 Complete the names of the clothes. Listen and check.

0 b e l t
1 _ _ e _ _
2 _ u _ e _
3 _ _ o e _
4 _ _ a i _ e _ _
5 _ o o _ _
6 _ a _ _ e _
7 _ _ i _ _
8 _ _ o _ _ _
9 _ _ o u _ e _ _

2 Answer the questions.

1 What are you wearing now?
2 What do you usually wear at weekends?
3 What do you never wear?
4 What clothes do you really like/dislike buying?

3 SPEAKING Work in pairs. Ask and answer the questions in Exercise 2. Then work with another partner.

I'm wearing a green shirt and jeans.

I never wear shorts.

→ workbook page 20

READING

4 🔊 2.08 Read and listen to the texts. Who likes:

1 reading?
2 visiting museums?
3 writing?
4 walking?

5 Think of three things you can do on a Sunday afternoon that are free. Write them down.

6 SPEAKING Work in pairs or small groups. Compare your ideas from Exercise 5.

It's Sunday afternoon
what can I do?

👤 Annie 7 May

It's Sunday afternoon. The last hours of the weekend before school starts again. This time is valuable, but I'm sitting here with nothing to do and no money to spend! So I need ideas for things to do. Important: they need to be fun and free. I'm asking for help because time is running out!

Austin08 (Five minutes ago)
Go for a walk. I always go for a walk on Sunday. I like going on my own. It's the perfect time to think about all the things I don't normally have time to think about and I never think about things I need to do. I like forgetting all about them just for a few hours every week.

MonsterMunch4342 (20 minutes ago)
I'm writing my weekly poetry blog post. Well, I was – now I'm writing to you. I upload a post every Sunday. At the moment, I'm finishing poem number 15. Five more to go! Maybe you don't want to write a poem or even a blog, so try a story. Go on – use your imagination!

Cool656Carl (25 minutes ago)
I'm lucky. I live in Liverpool and we have the best museums and they're all free. They're too big for just one visit, so one Sunday every month I go and check out a different room. Today it's the insect room – I want to see what unusual bugs they have!

SillyMilly (32 minutes ago)
Read something. Sunday is my reading day. I read for at least four hours on a Sunday – books, magazines, websites, newspapers – anything. It's free and best of all – you can do it anywhere. And sometimes, when I'm really lucky, Dad brings me a drink, too.

SPENDING MONEY UNIT 2

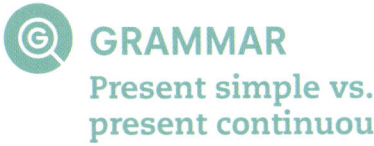

GRAMMAR
Present simple vs. present continuous

7 Look at the examples. Complete the rule.

present simple
I **upload** a post every Sunday.
I always **go** for a walk on Sunday.
I **read** for at least four hours on a Sunday.

present continuous
I'm **writing** my weekly poetry blog post.
I'm **sitting** here with nothing to do.
I'm **asking** for help.

> **RULE:** Use the ¹_____ to talk about habits, routines and things which are generally or always true.
> Use the ²_____ to talk about temporary things which are happening around the moment of speaking.

8 Match the sentences with the pictures. Write 1–4 in the boxes.

1 She paints well.
2 She's painting well.
3 He plays tennis.
4 He's playing tennis.

A

C

B

D

Look

These verbs are almost never used in the present continuous:

| believe | hate | know | like | mean |
| need | remember | understand | want |

I **know** the answer. (Not: I'm knowing the answer.)
I **understand** the problem.
(Not: I am understanding the problem.)

9 Choose the correct options.

1 We *always wear / 're always wearing* a uniform to school.
2 Natalia *wears / is wearing* black jeans today.
3 Come inside! It *rains / 's raining*.
4 It *doesn't rain / 's not raining* a lot in February.
5 Dad *cooks / 's cooking* at the moment.
6 My grandad *cooks / 's cooking* lunch every Sunday.
7 Dan's terrible! He *never listens / 's never listening* to the teacher!
8 Can you be quiet, please? I *listen / 'm listening* to some music.

10 Complete the sentences. Use the present simple or present continuous form of the verbs.

0 Ava usually ____*goes*____ (go) to school on her bike, but today she ____*is walking*____ (walk).
1 We _____ (have) science lessons three times a week. This week we _____ (learn) about trees.
2 Jason _____ (do) some shopping this afternoon. He _____ (want) to buy a new camera.
3 I _____ (know) her face, but I _____ (not remember) her name.
4 Ethan _____ (not watch) the game tonight because he _____ (not like) football.
5 What _____ this word _____ (mean)? I _____ (not understand) it.

→ workbook page 19

SPEAKING

11 Look at the photos. Who are the people in each one?

12 Work in pairs. Discuss the questions.

For each person, say …
• who they are.
• what they do.
• what they are doing.

> It's Kate Middleton. She's a …
> She's …

25

TH!NK
Banknotes

Culture

BANKNOTES

1 Look at the photos. Where can you see:
- a leader of a country
- a gate
- a jaguar

2 🔊 2.09 Read and listen to the article. Match the photos with the countries.

These days, we use credit cards more and more and they all look almost identical. But money is still with us, in coins and banknotes. The designs are different and all over the world we can see examples of really interesting and beautiful banknotes. The designs usually celebrate the country – its history, its geography, its animals and birds. Here are some examples of banknotes from different parts of the world.

Mexico

In Mexico the currency is the peso. The smallest banknote is 20 pesos, and the biggest is 1,000 pesos. One side always has the face of a famous person from Mexican history and the other side has well-known places in the country. On the $500 note there is a portrait of the famous Mexican artist Frida Kahlo. **1**

Turkey

In Turkey the currency is the Turkish lira, and there are six different banknotes. Each one shows Kemal Atatürk, the founder of the Turkish republic, on the front side, and another famous figure from Turkish history on the other side. **3**

Europe

Many countries in Europe use the euro, but the banknotes are exactly the same for each country. On one side, there is a picture of a gate, window or entrance, and on the other side, a bridge. The pictures represent different kinds of architecture from all over Europe. **2**

Brazil

The currency in Brazil is the real (plural, reais). The notes are in different colours, but they all have a picture of the Effigy of the Republic (a national symbol of Brazil) on one side, and various animals, birds and fish on the other side. One of the most beautiful is perhaps the R$50 note, which has a picture of a jaguar. **4**

A ☐ B ☐ C ☐

SPENDING MONEY　UNIT 2

3 **VOCABULARY** There are eight highlighted words in the article. Match the words with these meanings. Write the words.

0 the money of the country — *currency*
1 show _____
2 a picture of someone's head _____
3 a period of time in the past _____
4 exactly the same _____
5 famous _____
6 different types of _____
7 someone who starts a country _____

4 Read the article again. Correct the information in these sentences.

0 Most credit cards look different.
   Most credit cards look the same.
1 Mexican notes range from 200 to 1,000 pesos.
   _____
2 Frida Kahlo was a famous Mexican actor.
   _____
3 Euro banknotes are different in different countries.
   _____
4 In Turkey they use the dollar.
   _____
5 Brazilian banknotes have famous buildings on them.
   _____

SPEAKING

5 Work in pairs. Try and remember what's on the banknotes of your country, and any other countries you know. Compare your ideas with another pair.

WRITING
An email to say what you're doing

1 **INPUT** Read the email from Theo to his friend Azra. Answer the questions.

1 Where is Theo and what is he doing?
2 Where are his father and sister?
3 What is Theo's family doing this afternoon?

2 How does Theo start his email? And how does he finish it? Complete the table with the words in the list.

Dear | Love | Hello | See you soon | Best wishes

starting an email	ending an email
Hi (Azra),	Hope you're OK.
1_____ (Mike)	Bye
2_____ (Mr Jones)	3_____
	4_____
	5_____

3 **ANALYSE** Look at paragraphs 1 and 2 of Theo's email. Match the functions with the paragraphs. Write a–d.

Paragraph 1: __ and __ .
Paragraph 2: __ and __ .

a saying what you are doing
b talking about your plans
c saying where you are
d a description of the place where you are

4 Tick (✓) the things Theo writes about in his email.

1 what he likes about the city ☐
2 when he is coming home ☐
3 his plans for this afternoon ☐
4 where he is staying ☐
5 what his mother/father/sister are doing ☐
6 how Azra is ☐

5 **PRODUCE** Write an email to a friend (about 100–120 words). Imagine you are in a café or shop in a shopping centre. Use the example email and language above to help you.

Azra
Azra10@email.co.uk

Hello from Madrid!

Hi Azra,

(1) How are things with you? I'm in Madrid right now – we're here on holiday. Madrid is a really cool place. There are lots of great things to see and do here – shops, markets, and of course the football stadium! We're staying in a small hotel in the middle of Madrid and it's really nice.

(2) I'm sitting in a café at the moment, in the middle of the city. I'm here with my mum and we're having something to drink because it's really hot today! My dad and my sister are at a market near here – they're looking for some shoes for my sister. This afternoon we're visiting a museum of money. Don't ask why. It was Dad's suggestion.

(3) OK, my dad and sister are coming back, so I'm going now. Write soon and tell me how you are.
Hope you're OK.
Theo
PS I'm bringing you a 5 euro note home as a present. I hope you still collect banknotes!

27

A2 Key for Schools

READING AND WRITING
Part 1: 3-option multiple choice
→ workbook page 17

1 For each question, choose the correct answer.

A The boots are old.
B The boots are new.
C Phone in the morning.

A Ana is inviting Jen to Dave's party.
B Jen wants to lend Ana her red jacket.
C Ana wants to know if Jen needs her jacket.

A The shop is closed all day.
B Claire is getting married.
C You can visit the shop in the morning.

A Tom is in town.
B Ben is in a café.
C Ben wants to see Tom.

A They only have small T-shirts.
B The sale starts tomorrow.
C T-shirts are half price.

A Ian doesn't like his jeans anymore.
B Ian needs to call Ollie if he wants the jeans.
C The jeans are free.

Part 6: Writing – short message
→ workbook page 107

2 You want to go shopping with your friend Rory on Saturday. Write a message to Rory.

In your email:
- Ask Rory to go shopping with you.
- Say what shops you want to go to.
- Say where you want to meet.

Write 25 words or more.

LISTENING
→ workbook page 25

Part 1: 3-option multiple choice

3 🔊 2.10 For each question, choose the correct answer.

1 What are the girls talking about?

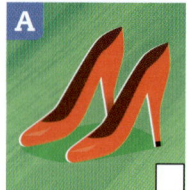  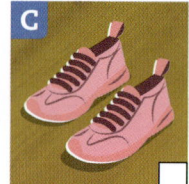

2 When does Oliver play tennis?

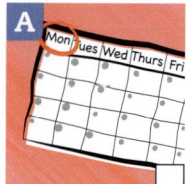 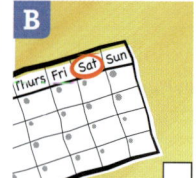 

3 Where is Brian?

4 What is Molly's hobby?

5 How much is the red jumper?

 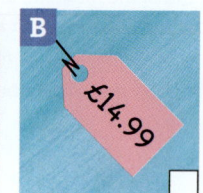 

TEST YOURSELF

UNITS 1 & 2

VOCABULARY

1 **Complete the sentences with the words in the list. There are two extra words.**

> belt | chemist's | club | collects | dress | jumper | plays
> shoe shop | sports shop | supermarket | take | write

1 I want to _____ a blog about food.
2 If you're cold, why don't you put on a _____ ?
3 Sara _____ the drums and the piano. She's really good at both.
4 I need to go to the _____ and buy a football.
5 My sister _____ old teddy bears. She's got more than 30!
6 I need some new boots. Let's go to the _____ .
7 I'm thinking about joining the tennis _____ , but it's very expensive.
8 Your trousers are falling down. You need a _____ .
9 Can you get some bread and some apples when you go to the _____ , please?
10 I always _____ lots of photos when I'm on holiday.

/10

GRAMMAR

2 **Complete the sentences with the words in the list.**

> 's working | 're writing | works | plays | 're playing | write

1 My brother's a cook. He _____ at a restaurant in town.
2 I like poetry. I _____ a poem every day.
3 Mum's in her office. She _____ on something very important.
4 Ollie's in a band. He _____ the guitar.
5 John and Camilla are on the computer. They _____ their blog.
6 Paul and Ryan are in the garden. They _____ football.

3 **Find and correct the mistake in each sentence.**

1 I can't stand to eat tomatoes.
2 We don't playing very well today.
3 They doesn't like watching TV.
4 That cake is tasting very good.
5 Does you speak German?
6 She goes always to the cinema at the weekend.

/12

FUNCTIONAL LANGUAGE

4 **Write the missing words.**

1 A Be _____ ! It looks very dangerous.
  B Don't worry. I'm _____ fun.
2 A How _____ do you play computer games?
  B _____ day when I get home from school.
3 A Look _____ ! There's a dog coming.
  B And it _____ look happy. Run!
4 A Please _____ shout! I've got a headache.
  B Oh, OK. I'm _____ .

/8

MY SCORE /30

22–30 | 10–21 | 0–9

29

3 WE ARE WHAT WE EAT

OBJECTIVES

FUNCTIONS:
apologising; talking about food; ordering a meal

GRAMMAR:
countable and uncountable nouns; *a/an*, *some*, *any*; *(how) much / (how) many*, *a lot of / lots of*; *too* and *(not) enough*

VOCABULARY:
food and drink; adjectives to talk about food; expressions with *have got*

Get TH!NKING

Watch the video and think: how does what we eat affect our health and the environment?

A _____

B _____

C _____

D _____

E _____

F _____

READING

1 Name the food in the pictures. What other food and drink words do you know in English?

2 Make sentences that are true for you. Compare your ideas in class.

I	always	have ... for	breakfast.
	often		lunch.
	sometimes		dinner.
	never		

3 Look at the photos on page 31. What do they show? Ask your teacher for the words you don't know. Then answer the questions.

Can you think of a food that ...

- comes from another country?
- has got a lot of vitamins?
- is (not) very healthy?
- is unusual for you?
- is good for your muscles and bones?

4 🔊 3.01 Read and listen to the article. Match the sentence halves.

0 The number of people in the world is — c
1 A lot of people
2 Farms cover about
3 It takes a lot of water and energy
4 Insects can help
5 They are healthy because
6 Many people don't know that

a one third of land.
b they've got protein in them.
c increasing very fast.
d some food colouring comes from a beetle.
e eat unhealthy food.
f to produce the meat people eat.
g with our problem.

5 **SPEAKING** Think about your answers to the questions below. Then work in pairs and compare your ideas. Do you agree?

- Do you think about the planet when you choose what you eat?
- Would you eat insects? Why (not)?
- What foods from your country are perhaps unusual for other people?
- What impact do your choices make?

WE ARE WHAT WE EAT   UNIT 3

Creepy-Crawlies
the superfood of the future?

The number of people in the world is growing fast – every year there are about 70 million more people. So, we've got two questions that need answers: Have we got enough space on our planet for so many people? and How can we make sure they've all got enough food to live?

Many people eat too much meat – steaks, beef burgers, sausages, etc. That's not good for us and we need big farms to produce all that meat. The farms already use 30% of all the world's land: they create greenhouse gases and use a lot of water and energy. However, we can do something to help. We can eat meat only one or two days a week, for example, and eat more vegetables – that's healthy. We can also eat some different types of meat – creepy-crawlies! That's right, grasshoppers, worms, flies and lots of other insects. They're the superfood of the future. They've got a lot of protein. Protein is very important for our health, and it's good for our hair and our skin.

Protein keeps our muscles and bones in good condition, too.
There are two more reasons why insects are good food options: insect farms don't need so much water and energy. Also, they don't use so much space.
For some people in countries in Asia and Latin America, eating insects is not unusual. But for people in Europe and many other countries, it seems very strange.

What about you? Do you eat any healthy food? How much meat do you eat in a week? Perhaps you think you don't eat insects? But maybe you're wrong! Why's that? Because the red food colouring that is in many things that we eat comes from … an insect called the 'cochineal beetle'!

 Like 47   Comment 3   Share 101

TH!NK values

Food and health

6 Complete the five conversations. Choose the correct answer A, B or C.

1 Do you want some ice cream?
   A No, thanks. Can I have an apple or a banana?
   B She's not hungry.
   C They're very good.
2 Have some water.
   A I drink it.
   B No, thanks, I'm not thirsty.
   C Look at them.
3 Would you like more chocolate?
   A It's over there.
   B Yes, I do.
   C I'd love some, but I'm trying not to eat it.

4 Do you eat any vegetables?
   A I hate apples.
   B It's fast food.
   C No, I don't like them.
5 Have some more biscuits.
   A Thanks, but one's enough for me.
   B You can have a banana.
   C I'm very healthy.

7 **SPEAKING** Work in pairs. Compare your answers. Do the people in Exercise 6 care about healthy food?

The person in number 1 | doesn't want a … | He/She asks for …
 | likes … | He/She says …
 | never eats / drinks … | He/She wants …

I think he/she | cares about …
 | doesn't care about …

31

VOCABULARY
Food and drink

1 🔊 3.02 Write the names of the food under the pictures. Listen and check.

2 **SPEAKING** Work in pairs. Ask and answer questions to find out three things from Exercise 1 your partner likes and doesn't like.

→ workbook page 30

GRAMMAR
Countable and uncountable nouns

3 Read the sentences.
   1 Can I have a carrot?
   2 I don't like rice.
   3 I don't like peppers.

   Choose the correct words in the rule.

   > **RULE:** Nouns that you can count (*one carrot*, *two carrots*, etc.) are ¹*countable / uncountable* nouns. Nouns you cannot count are ²*countable / uncountable nouns*. They have no plural forms.

4 Look at the photos in Exercise 1. Which are countable and which are uncountable? Add three more things to the lists.

a/an, some, any

5 Complete the sentences with *a/an*, *some* and *any*. Then choose the correct words in the rule.
   1 A Would you like _____ coffee?
      B No, thanks. I've got _____ tea.
   2 Can I have _____ apple or _____ banana?
   3 Have _____ biscuits.
   4 Are there _____ peppers in the kitchen?
   5 There isn't _____ yogurt in the fridge.

   > **RULE:** Use *a/an* with ¹*singular / plural* countable nouns.
   > Use *some* with ²*singular / plural* countable and uncountable nouns.
   > Use *any* in questions and in ³*positive / negative* sentences.
   > Use *some* in questions when offering or asking for something.

6 Complete the text with *a/an*, *some* and *any*.

   Do you like pancakes? They are easy to make! All you need is ¹_____ milk and flour and ²_____ egg! You also need ³_____ frying pan and ⁴_____ oil to fry them. After you make the pancakes, you can put ⁵_____ ice cream on top! Do you know ⁶_____ easy recipes?

   → workbook page 28

1 _____

6 _____

2 _____

7 _____

3 _____

8 _____

4 _____

9 _____

5 _____

10 _____

(how) much / (how) many, a lot of / lots of

7 Look at the examples. Complete the rule.

How much meat do you eat?	How many people eat insects?
I don't drink **much** coffee.	We haven't got **many** carrots.
Farms use **a lot of** water.	For **a lot of** people eating insects is not unusual.
Insects have got **lots of** protein.	We can eat **lots of** creepy-crawlies.

> **RULE:** We usually use *(how) much* and *(how) many* in questions and negative sentences.
> Use *many* with plural ¹_____ nouns and *much* with ²_____ nouns.
> Use *a lot of / lots of* with both countable and uncountable ³_____ .

WE ARE WHAT WE EAT UNIT 3

8 Complete the questions with *much* or *many*. Then match the questions (1–6) with the answers (a–f).
1 ☐ How _____ apples do you want?
2 ☐ How _____ sugar is in an avocado?
3 ☐ Are there _____ boys in your class?
4 ☐ How _____ peppers are there?
5 ☐ How _____ time have you got?
6 ☐ Have you got _____ homework?

a I think there are about five.
b Just one, please.
c Only 10 minutes.
d No, I haven't.
e I have no idea. I don't think it's a lot.
f Yes, there are 12, and 5 girls.

→ workbook page 28

LISTENING

9 🔊 3.03 Complete the menu with words from the list. Listen and check.

apple | cheese | chicken | chocolate
coffee | mushroom | potato | tea

LUNCH STOP

ROLLS/SANDWICHES:
2 fillings £4.50
Extra fillings 50p
- Tomato
- Tuna
- ¹_____
- Curried ²_____
- Sweet corn

SOUP (WITH BREAD): £4
- Chicken and ³_____
- ⁴_____ and onion
- Spicy red pepper

CAKES: £2
- Carrot
- ⁵_____
- ⁶_____ and walnut

DRINKS: £1.50
- Orange juice
- ⁷_____ juice
- ⁸_____
- Coffee
- Hot chocolate

10 🔊 3.04 Steve and Hannah are in Lunch Stop. Listen and write what they eat and drink.
Steve: _____
Hannah: _____

11 🔊 3.04 Listen again. Answer the questions.
1 What does Steve say about his roll?
2 What does Hannah say about her soup?
3 Why does Hannah need a fork?

12 🔊 3.05 Complete the dialogue with *all, altogether, change, help, milk, minutes, please* and *something*. Then listen and check.

Café assistant: Customer:

Good morning. Can I
¹_____ you?
                        → I'd like some coffee, please.
Do you want
²_____ or sugar?
                        → Just milk, ³_____ .
Would you like
⁴_____ to eat?
                        → Yes, I'd like a cheese and mushroom omelette, please.
Is that ⁵_____ ?
                        → Oh, I'd like a carrot juice, too, please.
That's £9
⁶_____ .
                        → Here you are.
Here's your
⁷_____ . Your breakfast will be ready in a few ⁸_____ .
                        → Thank you.

13 **SPEAKING** Work in groups of three. One is the café assistant; the others are customers. Order meals.
Use the menu in Exercise 9 and the language in Exercise 12.

PRONUNCIATION
Vowel sounds: /ɪ/ and /iː/ Go to page 120. 🎧

WordWise: have got

14 Put the words in order to make sentences.
1 got / cakes / some / They've / great
2 I've / Don't / reasons / worry / my / got
3 that / a / problem / got / you / Have / with

15 Complete with the expressions from the list.

~~a problem~~ | my reasons | a headache
time | something to do

0 A I've got _a problem_ with my homework.
  B History? Sorry! I can't help you.
1 A Are you OK?
  B I've got _____ . It hurts.
2 A Why are you not inviting Jane to your party?
  B I've got _____ , but I don't want to tell you.
3 A Phil, can you help me, please?
  B Sorry. I'm busy. I haven't got _____ .
4 A Let's go to town tomorrow.
  B Sorry, no, I've got _____ tomorrow.

→ workbook page 30

33

READING

1 Read the article quickly and answer the questions.
1 Where is the writer?
2 Why is it difficult to get vegetables there?
3 What do the Inuits eat a lot of?

2 🔊 3.08 Read and listen to the article and answer the questions.
1 Why is the writer staying in an Inuit village?
2 What other food apart from meat can the people find there?
3 What is the problem with growing vegetables there?
4 What is surprising about the Inuits' health situation?

WRITING
What you eat

3 INPUT Match the sentence halves and read Matt Silver's paragraph about what 15-year-old Amanda eats.

1 Hello, I'm Matt Silver and today I'm _d_
2 Amanda has lots of choices __
3 There are many good __
4 Amanda tries to eat __
5 She likes fruit __
6 She sometimes eats meat, __
7 Amanda loves fish, __
8 There is only one little problem with Amanda's food choices; __

a shops and restaurants.
b but not too much.
c a lot of healthy food.
d writing about 15-year-old Amanda Claxton.
e and that's very healthy.
f she loves sweets, but she tries not to eat too many.
g for food here.
h and vegetables.

4 Write out the paragraph in your notebooks.

5 PRODUCE Imagine Matt Silver is writing about what you eat. What is healthy or unhealthy about your food? What do you eat too much / not enough of? Write Matt's paragraph.

EATING around the world

Matt

Part I: The Inuits

Hello, I'm Matt Silver, and this is an article from our new series 'Eating around the world'.

I'm writing this from Kulusuk, an Inuit village in Greenland. It's a pleasant place in summer, with mild temperatures and fantastic views of the icebergs on the sea just in front of the village.

It's a popular place for tourists in those months. But winters are long and hard, and the life for the 250 people in the village isn't easy at all. The roads are covered in ice, and the sea is frozen, too.

The Inuits don't have a lot of choices for food. The summer is too short and not long enough for the Inuits to grow vegetables. They sometimes find berries during the warmer months. And they eat seaweed. But there are no other vegetables, so they don't eat enough greens. There is a shop in the village, but during the winter it doesn't get any fresh vegetables.

This is why the Inuits eat lots of raw and boiled meat. They eat sea animals – seals, whales and fish – and they eat reindeer and other land animals. These animals have a lot of fat on them because it keeps them warm in the freezing temperatures. Do the Inuits eat too much fat? Isn't that very dangerous?

Well, here's the surprise: in the western world, people say 'Don't eat too much fat!' But the Inuits eat a lot of animal fat and they are healthy, perhaps because they eat boiled rather than fried meat. Life for the people from Kulusuk can be difficult but they are healthy. Maybe we can learn a lot from them!

WE ARE WHAT WE EAT UNIT 3

GRAMMAR
too many/much, (not) enough + noun

6 **Choose the correct word and complete the rule.**

1 I try not to eat too *much / many* sweets.
2 He eats too *much / many* fat.
3 They don't eat *much / enough* greens.
4 There are too *many / much* people in the city.
5 She doesn't eat *many / enough* meat.

> RULE: Use *too* ¹_____
> with countable nouns, and *too*
> ² _____ with uncountable nouns.
> Use (*not*) *enough* with ³_____
> and ⁴_____ .

7 **Complete with *too much*, *too many* or *not enough*.**

1 There are _____ onions on this pizza. I don't like them.
2 There's _____ salt in this soup. I can't eat it.
3 There is _____ sugar in my coffee. Can I have some more, please?
4 There are _____ cars on the road. It's dangerous to ride my bike.
5 We've got _____ homework tonight. I want to watch TV.
6 There are _____ chairs. Can you stand?

too + adjective, (not +) adjective + enough

8 **Use the example sentences to choose the correct words in the rule.**

The winters are too long there.
The summers are not long enough.

> RULE: We use *too* + adjective to say that something is ¹*more / less* than we like or want.
> We use *not* + adjective + *enough* to say that something is ²*more / less* than we like or want.

9 **Complete the sentences.**

0 The test is too easy. It's ___*not hard enough*___ .
1 The film isn't exciting enough. It's _____ .
2 The T-shirt is too expensive. It's _____ .
3 It's not warm enough today. It's _____ .
4 Your bike's too small for me. It's _____ .
5 His car's not fast enough. It's _____ .

10 **Complete with *not enough* or *too*.**

My dad always says there's ¹_____ much rain in the UK in the summer, and that it's ²_____ hot _____. He's right. And I feel that it's ³_____ boring to spend holidays here. We usually go to the south of Italy for our holidays. There are lots of beaches, so there are never ⁴_____ many tourists. I love the food; that's why I often eat ⁵_____ much.

→ workbook page 29

VOCABULARY
Adjectives to talk about food

11 **Write the adjectives under the photos.**

> boiled | fried | grilled | roast

A  B  C  D

_____ _____ _____ _____

12 **Put the words in the list in order from 'very good' to 'very bad'.**

> (a bit) boring | delicious | horrible | nice

13 **SPEAKING** Work in pairs. Ask and answer questions. Use the words from Exercise 12.

> boiled or roast beef? | grilled or fried chicken? | boiled or roast potatoes? boiled or fried eggs? | grilled or fried fish?

What do you prefer, boiled or roast beef?

Roast beef. It's delicious

Look

Savoury means not sweet, for example, salty or spicy. *Savoury* is a positive adjective. *Salty* is a negative adjective, meaning food has too much salt.

14 **How do you say these words in your language? Write two types of food for each category.**

> delicious | disgusting | fatty | fresh | salty
> savoury | spicy | sweet | tasty | yummy

sweet: chocolate, strawberries

→ workbook page 30

35

DEVELOPING SPEAKING

1 🔊 3.09 Look at the photo. What food is it? How do you know? Listen and read to check.

Dad: Hi, Jordan! I'm home.
Jordan: Hi, Dad!
Dad: So, what are you doing?
Jordan: I'm making pizza – for me and my friends.
Dad: Hmmm … ¹What about me?
Jordan: I'm really sorry, Dad, it's just for us.
Dad: Oh right. Look at this kitchen! What a mess!
Jordan: Sorry, Dad. But don't worry. I'm finishing now!
Dad: OK then. Now, how can I help?
Jordan: ²Actually, I'm OK. It's just a pizza.
Dad: Onion? Red pepper? Just that? We can make that better, I'm sure.
Jordan: Really?
Dad: Let's add ³a couple of mushrooms. There we are.
Jordan: But I don't like mushrooms.
Dad: ⁴So what? You can always take them off. I think you need some chilli pepper ⁵as well.
Jordan: Dad, stop it. It's horrible. Thanks a lot.
Dad: Are you ⁶upset with me? Now I feel bad. I just wanted to help.
Jordan: Don't worry, Dad. We can just eat crisps.
Dad: No, you can't. You can eat pizza. Get me the phone and I'll order one. Ice cream, too!
Jordan: Really, Dad? Thanks!
Dad: And I can eat this one here!

2 🔊 3.09 Read and listen again and answer the questions.
1 What is Jordan doing?
2 Who is he making it for?
3 What does his dad put on the pizza?
4 What does Jordan decide to give his friends?
5 What does his dad offer to do?

Phrases for fluency

3 Match the underlined expressions (1–6) in the dialogue to the definitions (a–f).
a too – *as well*
b unhappy with – _____
c one or two (but not many) – _____
d What is the situation (for me)? – _____
e In fact, – _____
f Why is that a problem? – _____

4 Use the expressions from Exercise 3 to complete the mini-dialogues.
1 **A** Mum? John's got his sandwiches. But _____ me?
   B Well, I'm making _____ cheese and tomato sandwiches for you right now.
   A Cool! Can I have an apple _____ ?
2 **A** I broke your watch. I'm sorry. Are you _____ me?
   B Don't worry about it. _____ , it wasn't very good.
3 **A** I can't go to the cinema. I've got homework.
   B _____ ? You can do it at the weekend.

⚙ FUNCTIONS
Apologising

5 Look at the phrases. When and why might you use them?

> **KEY LANGUAGE**
> 1 I'm really sorry.
> 2 I feel really bad.
> 3 Don't worry.
> 4 It's OK.

6 🔊 3.10 Complete the dialogue with words from the Key Language box. Listen and check. Then act it out in pairs.

Man Oh no. I'm really ¹_____ .
Woman ²_____ worry. It's not my favourite picture.
Man But it's broken. I ³_____ really bad.
Woman ⁴_____ OK. Really. I don't really like it anyway.

7 In pairs write a short dialogue for the picture. Act it out.

UNIT 3

LIFE COMPETENCIES

We all make mistakes. We say we're sorry so that the person feels better and understands that we care. Saying sorry is important, but sometimes we also need to show we are sorry by our actions.

Saying sorry

1 ▶ 09 Watch the vlog. What are the names of Jack's brother and sister?

2 ▶ 09 Watch again and complete the sentences.

We all make ¹_____ .
Saying 'sorry' helps make things ²_____ .
When you say sorry, you should mean it.
A ³_____ sorry is worse than no sorry (probably).
A good sorry says three things:
- I am ⁴_____ .
- It's my ⁵_____ .
- How can I make things ⁶_____ ?
Is sorry really the ⁷_____ word? Probably not.

3 Read these situations. Who do you think needs to say sorry and why?

A Tom arrives late to school for the second time in a week. The teacher gives him a detention.
Tom needs to say sorry because he's late.

B Abby's dad calls her lazy because she never tidies her bedroom.

C Zoe forgets her friend's birthday. The next day, her friend doesn't speak to her.

D Emily is wearing her new shoes. Amy says they look terrible. Emily is upset and tells her friends not to speak to Amy.

E George orders a cheese and onion pizza. The waiter brings him a tuna and pepper pizza.

F Kevin's mum asks him to watch her cake in the oven. He forgets and it burns.

4 Work in pairs. Compare your answers to Exercise 3. Do you agree?

5 SPEAKING Work in pairs. Discuss which of these things is a good idea for the people in Exercise 3. More than one answer is possible.

- Can you think of other ways of apologising?
- Say sorry immediately.
- Say 'I'm here for you'.
- Change our future actions.
- Be quiet.
- Write a short letter or card to say sorry.
- Say something funny.
- Buy a present or flowers.
- Wait and say sorry later.
- Say 'I love you!' and smile.

6 Work in pairs. Write a situation similar to the ones in Exercise 3 where someone needs to apologise.

7 SPEAKING Read your situation to the rest of the class. Discuss these questions:
1 Who needs to say sorry?
2 What is the best way to say sorry?
3 What does the person saying sorry have to say? Do they need to do anything else?
4 How do you feel after you apologise?

Me and my world

8 Tick (✓) the sentences you agree with. Compare with a partner.
- [ ] I say sorry a lot.
- [ ] I find it difficult to say sorry.
- [ ] I don't always mean it when I say sorry.
- [ ] Sometimes sorry is not enough.
- [ ] Saying sorry solves a lot of problems.

TIPS FOR SAYING SORRY

- Don't be afraid to recognise when you make a mistake.
- Say sorry when you make a mistake. It shows that you care about others.
- Saying sorry isn't always enough. Sometimes you also have to change your actions.

4 ALL IN THE FAMILY

OBJECTIVES

FUNCTIONS:
talking about families; asking for permission

GRAMMAR:
possessive adjectives and pronouns; *whose* and possessive *'s*; *was* / *were*

VOCABULARY:
family members; feelings

Get TH!NKING
Watch the video and think: what is a 'family'?

READING

1 **Find the pairs of words.**

brother   daughter   father   husband
mother   sister   son   wife

2 **Choose two of the words in Exercise 1 to describe each person in the picture.**

The boy is a son and a brother.

3 **Work in pairs. Write as many examples as you can of:**
   1 a brother and sister from a film
   2 a husband and wife from a film

4 **SPEAKING** Compare your examples with another pair. Have you got the same ideas?

5 **4.01** Read and listen to the blog on page 39. Do they mention any of the families you talked about?

6 **Read the blog again. Correct the information in these sentences.**
   1 Emma thinks the second *Home Alone* film was the best.
   2 Kevin is sad when his family return home on Christmas morning.
   3 Only the parents in *The Incredibles* have superpowers.
   4 There are four members of the Parr family.
   5 The Addams children want to be in a normal family.
   6 Fester is Pugsley's father.

ALL IN THE FAMILY — UNIT 4

OLD FILMS, GREAT FAMILIES

I love old films and my family loves them, too. My mum and dad always talk about a really old film called *Swiss Family Robinson*, also a book, about a Swiss family who find themselves on a desert island when their boat sinks. And do you know what? I like it, too. So guys – here's today's topic. Old films about families. So you know my opinion, what about yours?

3 comments   reply to post   share

How about the *Home Alone* films in the 1990s, all about 8-year-old Kevin McCallister? The first one is definitely the best. Kevin's parents forget to take him on the family Christmas holiday. Kevin is happy at first because he's got the whole house to himself and his brothers and sisters aren't there to annoy him. He has lots of fun stopping two silly criminals from robbing the family home. But he starts to miss his family and on Christmas morning he gets the best present of all – everyone comes back home! It was funny then and it's still funny now.
Emma, Brighton

Whose favourite family is the Parrs in *The Incredibles*? Remember them? The Parrs are like most families. You know, they fight and argue and have fun. But they're also a family of superheroes. Dad is super strong. Mum is super stretchy. Violet, their eldest child, can turn invisible, and then nobody can see her. Her younger brother Dash is super fast and her baby brother Jack-Jack has laser eyes. I think those films are great, old or not.
Max, Birmingham

I like your comments, Max and Emma. And here is mine. *The Addams Family*! They're a really strange family who live in a normal town. They all wear black. They live in a huge old house. Other families think they're a little bit scary, but the Addams family don't care. The parents, Gomez and Morticia, and their children, Wednesday and Pugsley, are happy being different. And there's Cousin It, too. He (or she – no one is sure) is covered in fur. And finally there is Uncle Fester, Gomez's brother. They're one of the best loved screen families of all time – in my house, anyway!
Moira, Edinburgh

TH!NK values

Film families

7 Think about your favourite film family. Tick (✓) the things they do.

My favourite film family are _____ .
- They help each other. ☐
- They fight a lot. ☐
- They laugh a lot. ☐
- They spend a lot of time together. ☐
- They talk about their problems. ☐
- They are good friends. ☐

8 Make notes about your favourite film family. Are they a good family?

9 **SPEAKING** Work in small groups. Tell each other about your favourite film families, and decide together which one is the best.

The Incredibles are usually a good family because …

But sometimes they …

39

GRAMMAR
Possessive adjectives and pronouns

1 Complete the sentences with the words in the list. Look at the blog on page 39 and check your answers.

> my | mine | your | yours

1 So you know _____ opinion, what about _____?
2 I like _____ comments, Max and Emma. And here is _____.

2 Complete the rule with *pronouns* and *adjectives*. Then complete the table.

> **RULE:** Possessive ¹_____ come before a noun to show who something belongs to, e.g., It's *my* book. Possessive ²_____ can take the place of the possessive adjective and the noun, e.g., The book is *mine*.

possessive adjectives	possessive pronouns
0 It's _my_ book.	The book is _mine_.
1 It's your book.	The book is _____.
2 It's _____ book.	The book is hers.
3 It's _____ book.	The book is his.
4 It's our book.	The book is _____.
5 It's _____ book.	The book is theirs.

whose and possessive 's

Look

Be careful with *whose* and *who's*.
Whose = belongs to someone:
Whose tablet is this? = Who does this tablet belong to?
Who's = who + is:
Who's that person? = Who is that person?

3 Choose the correct words and complete the rule.

A ¹Whose / Who's favourite family is the Parrs?
B The Parrs are ²Max's / Maxs' favourite.
A ³Whose / Who's Violet's baby brother?
B Jack-Jack.

> **RULE:** To ask about possession, we use the question word ¹_____.
> To talk about possession, add ²_____ to the end of a name / noun.
> If the name / noun ends in an **-s**, we add an apostrophe (') after the **-s**.

4 Choose the correct words. Compare your answers with a partner.

1 A Whose / Who is this phone?
  B Ask Jenny. I think it's *her* / *hers*.
2 Hey! That's *my* / *mine* sandwich – not *your* / *yours*.
3 A Whose / Who do you sit next to in Maths?
  B Rashid / Rashid's.
4 A Is that your *parent's* / *parents'* dog?
  B Yes, I think it's *their* / *theirs*.

→ workbook page 36

VOCABULARY
Family members

5 Read the text. Complete the spaces in the picture with the missing family words.

> Here's a photo of my dad's side of the family. My dad's got a *big* brother called Bob. He's my *uncle* and he's great. He's so funny. His wife Jemma is my *aunt*, of course. She's also really nice. They've got two sons – Jimmy and his *little* brother Robin. They're my *cousins*. Jimmy is also my best friend. My dad and Bob have the same mum and dad. They are my *grandparents*. I call them *Grandma* Diana and *Grandpa* Roger. They're really nice to me because I'm their only *granddaughter*.

Dad's ¹_____ brother
My ²_____ Bob

My ³_____ Jemma

⁰*Grandpa* Roger

My dad

⁴_____ Diana

My ⁵_____ Jimmy

Jimmy's ⁶_____ brother (also my ⁷_____)

6 SPEAKING Work in pairs. How many sentences can you make about the family in two minutes?

Diana is Roger's wife.   *Jimmy is Jemma's son.*

→ workbook page 39

40

ALL IN THE FAMILY UNIT 4

🎧 LISTENING

A
B
C

7 Read and match three of the sentences with the pictures.

Why I love my family!

1 Mum always gives me lifts to parties. (Tom, 15)
2 Dad makes the best cooked breakfast at the weekend. (Eddie, 17)
3 My aunt takes us climbing on Saturdays. (Jason, 16)
4 My big sister Olivia lets me borrow her clothes. (Lori, 13)
5 My grandad tells the best jokes. He's so funny. (Chloe, 14)
6 My brother loves helping me with my Maths homework. (Becca, 14)

8 🔊 4.02 Listen to the dialogues. Who is talking?

Dialogue 1 – _____ and _____
Dialogue 2 – _____ and _____

9 🔊 4.02 Listen again and answer the questions. Compare your answers with a partner.

1 What is Lori looking for?
2 Where is she going?
3 What does Olivia say 'no' to?
4 When is Nathan's party?
5 How far away is Foxton?
6 What time does Tom need to leave the party?

PRONUNCIATION
-er /ə/ at the end of words Go to page 120. 🎧

⚙️ FUNCTIONS
Asking for permission

10 Complete the sentences from the listening.

Asking for permission	Saying yes	Saying no
¹_____ I borrow your red boots?	Of course you can.	No, you ²_____.

11 Think of requests that you make to different members of your family. Write them down. Use language from Exercise 10.

Can I borrow …?   Can I have …?

12 Read your requests to your partner. Can he/she guess who you say this to?

13 Write a short dialogue for the picture.

SUZIE SAVES HER MUM

One day Suzie McCash went shopping with her mum in Tynemouth, England. Suzie was four years old. Her mum didn't feel very well at the shops, so they went home.

In the house, Suzie's mum went to lie on the sofa. She was there for a long time. Her eyes were shut and it wasn't easy for her to breathe. Suzie was worried. Was her mum really ill? Suzie went to the house next door, but the neighbours weren't there. So she phoned 999 – the emergency telephone number for the police.

The police officer was very kind and Suzie was calm.

OFFICER: 'What's your mummy doing now?'
SUZIE: 'Um, she's just sitting on the sofa and she's doing nothing.'
OFFICER: 'Are her eyes open?'
SUZIE: 'No, they're shut.'

And later…
OFFICER: 'Can you open the door? Can you be a big girl?'

Soon the police were at their house and an ambulance was there, too. About an hour later, Suzie's mum was OK again. A doctor said: 'Her mummy was very sick. Without Suzie's phone call, her mummy might be dead now.'

Suzie's story was in the newspapers and people were surprised and happy about it. She was a very brave girl and, a year later, she was in the news again because she was named a Child of Courage at the Pride of Britain Awards for helping her mother.

READING

1 🔊 4.05 Look at the title. What do you think happened? Read and listen to the article and find out.

2 Read the article again. Put the sentences in the correct order. There is one event that is not in the article. Where do you think it goes?

a Suzie phones the police.
b The ambulance arrives.
c They come home from the shops.
d The police officer asks Suzie where she lives.
e Suzie's mum lies down on the sofa.

Train to TH!NK

Making inferences

3 Work in pairs. Who says these sentences? Mark them S (Suzie), P (police officer) or M (Mum).

1 'It's open.'
2 'Is she injured?'
3 'She's so amazing.'
4 'How can I help?'
5 'I can hear an ambulance.'
6 'How old are you?'

4 Work in pairs. Write one more thing for each person to say.

1 Suzie
2 The police officer
3 The ambulance driver
4 Suzie's mother

5 Read your sentences to another pair for them to guess.

I think Suzie says that.   *That's probably the police officer.*

ALL IN THE FAMILY   UNIT 4

Grammar rap! ▶11

GRAMMAR
was / were

6 Look at the examples from the article on page 42. Choose the correct words.
1 It *was / wasn't* easy for her mum to breathe.
2 *Was / Were* her mum really ill?
3 The neighbours *wasn't / weren't* there.
4 People *was / were* surprised and happy about it.

7 Complete the table.

Positive	Negative
I/he/she/it ⁰ _was_ .	I/he/she/it ¹ _____ (was not).
You/we/they ⁰ _were_ .	You/we/they ² _____ (were not).
Questions	**Short answers**
³ _____ I/he/she/it?	Yes, I/he/she/it ⁴ _____ . No, I/he/she/it ⁵ _____ .
⁶ _____ you/we/they?	Yes, you/we/they ⁷ _____ . No, you/we/they ⁸ _____ .

8 Complete the questions and answers with *was*, *were*, *wasn't* or *weren't*.
1 A _____ you in bed at 9 pm last night?
   B No, I _____ . I _____ in the kitchen with my mum and dad.
2 A _____ your teacher happy with your homework?
   B Yes, she _____ . She _____ very happy with it.
3 A _____ it hot yesterday?
   B No, it _____ . It _____ really cold.
4 A _____ we at school yesterday?
   B No, we _____ . It _____ Sunday!
5 A _____ your parents born in the UK?
   B No, they _____ . They _____ born in India.

9 **SPEAKING** Work in pairs. Ask and answer the questions in Exercise 8.

→ workbook page 37

VOCABULARY
Feelings

10 Match the sentences.
1 Our daughter was first in the race. ☐
2 It was 9 pm and Mum wasn't home. ☐
3 That wasn't a nice thing to say to Miriam. ☐
4 That Maths lesson was really difficult. ☐
5 I wasn't expecting a big party. ☐
6 The students were really noisy. ☐
7 It was a really good horror film. ☐
8 The test was really hard. ☐

a She's really **upset** now.
b And the teacher was **angry**.
c I was very **surprised** to see so many people there.
d I'm really **confused** now.
e We are so **proud** of her.
f I was **relieved** when it was over.
g I was a bit **worried**. Where was she?
h I was really **scared** at the end of it.

11 Match the sentences in Exercise 10 with the pictures. Write the numbers 1–8.

12 Add more words to the spider diagram for feelings.

feelings

→ workbook page 38

A B C D E F G H

43

Culture

TH!NK Family traditions around the world ▶12

1. Look at the photos. What do they show?
2. 🔊 4.06 Read and listen to the article. Write the names of the countries under the photos.
3. What family traditions are there in your country?

FAMILY TRADITIONS around the world

The idea of the family is important all over the world and many countries have special occasions to celebrate it. Let's look at a few …

FIRST DAY AT SCHOOL – GERMANY

In Germany, the first day at school is a very important time for all children. There is a special event called an *Einschulung*. Everyone in the family meets to give the child presents, like pens and books, for their new school life. For the first day of school, parents give their children a large paper cone called a *Schultüte*. Inside there are things for school and sweets.

REMEMBERING YOUR ANCESTORS – JAPAN

In traditional Japanese houses you often find a *butsudan*. A *butsudan* is a special place where you go to remember your dead relatives. People usually put things on the *butsudan* for their ancestors: a book, some flowers or a bowl of rice, for example. Adults also tell stories about these people to their children so they are not forgotten.

LOOKING AFTER ANIMALS – INDIA

Pets are popular in many cultures around the world. Looking after an animal helps a child learn how to be responsible. Every year in India there is a Hindu festival called *Thai Pongal*. During the festival families feed cows and birds to give thanks for these animals. Children also learn that all living things are connected and must share the world together.

WRITING POEMS – THE NETHERLANDS

In the Netherlands people celebrate the winter holiday on the 5th December. This holiday is called *Sinterklaas*. People give each other presents, but they also have a very special tradition. Each member of the family writes their name on a piece of paper and puts it in a hat. Everyone then takes a name from the hat and writes a poem about this person. Everyone sits in a circle and reads out their poems.

ALL IN THE FAMILY UNIT 4

4 Read the article again and answer the questions.
1 What is an *Einschulung*?
2 What can you find inside a *Schultüte*?
3 Where can you find a *butsudan*?
4 What is *Thai Pongal*?
5 When and where do people celebrate *Sinterklaas*?

5 Work in small groups. Talk about any special traditions your own families have.

We all have breakfast together at the local café on Sundays.

We usually spend the summer holidays at our grandparents' house.

I take my mum and dad a cup of tea in bed on Sunday mornings.

6 **VOCABULARY** There are six **highlighted** words in the article. Match the words with these meanings. Write the words.

0 to have fun, do something special, for example on a friend's birthday *celebrate*
1 something important or unusual that happens _____
2 to give food to _____
3 to have something at the same time with other people _____
4 the people in your family _____
5 something you give to a person on a special day _____

WRITING
An invitation

1 **INPUT** Read the emails. Answer the questions.
1 Who is Ella?
2 Can Daniel go to the party?

Jen
Jen_Walker@hooray.co.uk

Party!

Hi Daniel,
Would you like to come to my house on Saturday for a party at 8 pm? It's my cousin Ella's birthday.
My address is 43 Park Street. Can you make a playlist for the party? I love your music.
Hope you can come. Let me know soon.
Jen
PS Don't tell Ella. It's a surprise!

Daniel
DanielB@thinkmail.com

RE: Party!

Hi Jen,
I'd love to come to your party on Friday, but I've got a small problem. I've got theatre practice from 7 to 8 pm. Can I arrive a bit late? Is that OK?
No problem with the playlist. I've got some great new songs.
See you on Saturday.
Daniel

2 Match the sentences with the same meaning. Write a–e in the boxes.
a Would you like to come to my party?
b I'd love to come to your party.
c I'm sorry I can't come to your party.
d Make a playlist, please.
e Don't tell Ella.

☐ I don't want Ella to know.
☐ Can you make a playlist?
☐ Can you come to my party?
☐ I'd love to come, but I can't.
☐ I'd be very happy to accept your invitation.

3 **ANALYSE** Which pairs of sentences in Exercise 2 can you use to do these things?
1 accept an invitation __
2 give an order __
3 make an invitation __
4 make a request __
5 refuse an invitation __

4 Read the invitation again and answer the questions.
1 What is the invitation for?
2 What special requests does Jen make?

5 **PLAN** You want to invite a friend to your house. What information should you include? Tick (✓) the correct answers.
☐ your address
☐ how many brothers and sisters you've got
☐ the time you want them to come
☐ the reason
☐ who your favourite singer is
☐ the day or date you want them to come

6 **PRODUCE** Write an invitation to a friend. Choose one of these reasons. Include a special request or instruction. (50 words)
• It's your birthday.
• You've got a great new series online to watch.
• You've got a new computer game.

A2 Key for Schools

READING AND WRITING
Part 2: 3-option multiple choice
→ workbook page 35

1 For each question, choose the correct answer.

MEET SOME YOUNG SPORTS STARS

A AMY

My parents love sports. My mum was in her college volleyball team, and my dad plays ice hockey. We do a lot of sports together: swimming, climbing and cycling. My favourite is swimming. I practise every day from 6 to 7 am, and now I'm in my college's team. My dream is to be really good and to swim in the Olympic Games.

B BARBARA

My brother and I live with our mum. She isn't very interested in sports, but she's happy that we like them. I love skiing and now it's the only thing I want to do! It's an expensive sport, but at the weekends, I work in a shop in town. This way I can save a lot of money to buy equipment, go to the mountains and practise. I hope to be in the national ski team one day.

C CINDY

I'm tall like my father and my uncle. My dad wants me to play basketball, but I think I prefer running. My uncle was a very good runner, and I'm good, too – but I can't run long distances like he did when he was young! I'm a good basketball player, too, so right now I'm trying to decide: basketball or running? It's difficult, but I have to choose one.

		Amy	Barbara	Cindy
1	Who has a job so she is able to do her sport?	A	B	C
2	Who travels to another place to practise her sport?	A	B	C
3	Who does sport with her parents?	A	B	C
4	Who doesn't do the sport a parent wants her to do?	A	B	C
5	Who gets up early to practise?	A	B	C
6	Who has parents who like sports a lot?	A	B	C
7	Who has a problem about which sport to do?	A	B	C

Part 4: 3-option multiple choice cloze
→ workbook page 89

2 For these questions, choose the correct answer for each gap.

Pelé: the star

It is ¹_____ 1958. In Solna, Sweden, it is a semifinal of the World Cup between Brazil and France. Brazil's 17-year-old player, Edson Arantes do Nascimento, gets three goals and his team ²_____ the match. People now ³_____ him as Pelé, and he is the youngest player to play in the 1958 World Cup. In the final match, Brazil wins against Sweden, 5–2, and this ⁴_____ Pelé scores twice.

Now ⁵_____ in the world knows his name. In 1962, Brazil win the World Cup again, but without Pelé, because he hurt himself. But in 1970 in Mexico, Brazil and Pelé are the world's best ⁶_____ .

In 92 games for Brazil, Pelé scores 77 goals. He is one of the country's great sports people.

1	A 9 am	B Sunday	C June
2	A starts	B wins	C makes
3	A know	B call	C say
4	A time	B moment	C hour
5	A people	B all	C everyone
6	A again	B new	C more

LISTENING
Part 3: 3-option multiple choice
→ workbook page 43

3 🔊 4.07 For each question, choose the correct answer. You will hear Jackie talking to her friend Oliver about his family.

1 The party was for Oliver's
 A brother. B dad. C uncle.

2 The party was Friday
 A evening. B morning. C afternoon.

3 Oliver's aunt is called
 A Anna. B Carla. C Ruth.

4 Mike is Oliver's
 A brother. B dad. C cousin.

5 Oliver has got
 A one sister. B two sisters. C one brother.

TEST YOURSELF

UNITS 3 & 4

VOCABULARY

1 **Complete the sentences with the words in the list. There are two extra words.**

> angry | big | boiled | carrots | chicken | confused
> grandparents | grilled | proud | relieved | scared | spicy

1 I don't like many vegetables – just peppers and _____ .
2 I was really worried about the exam, so I was _____ when it was over.
3 The curry is too _____ . I can't eat it.
4 It was a really silly thing to do. My parents were really _____ with me.
5 To make _____ potatoes, you need to cook them in water for about 20 minutes.
6 There was a strange noise outside the house. We were a bit _____ .
7 Ali's a vegetarian. She doesn't eat _____ .
8 I don't really understand this homework. I'm a bit _____ .
9 Freddie's my _____ brother. I'm 14 and he's 20.
10 My mum's mother and father are my _____ .

/10

GRAMMAR

2 **Complete the sentences with the words in the list.**

> many | much | our | ours | was | were

1 How _____ sugar do you want in your coffee?
2 It _____ really cold yesterday.
3 That's not your cat, it's _____ .
4 There are too _____ socks on your bedroom floor!
5 _____ rabbit's called Spike.
6 Where _____ you last night?

3 **Find and correct the mistake in each sentence.**

1 This salad has got too much beans.
2 That's not your sandwich. It's my.
3 My parents was very proud of my school report.
4 I like Kate and I really like hers sister too.
5 How many water do you want?
6 I think this is Kevins' book.

/12

FUNCTIONAL LANGUAGE

4 **Write the missing words.**

1 A I'm late. I'm really _____ .
  B Don't _____ . We've still got lots of time.
2 A I _____ this question is really difficult.
  B I think _____ , too.
3 A _____ I borrow your bike, Dad?
  B Of _____ you can.
4 A Can I go _____ tonight?
  B No, you _____ .

/8

MY SCORE /30

22–30   10–21   0–9

5 NO PLACE LIKE HOME

OBJECTIVES

FUNCTIONS: making and responding to suggestions; talking about events in the past

GRAMMAR: past simple (regular verbs); modifiers: *quite, very, really*; past simple negative

VOCABULARY: parts of a house and furniture; adjectives with *-ed / -ing*; phrasal verbs with *look*

Get TH!NKING
Watch the video and think: what does 'home' mean to you?

READING

1 🔊 5.01 Match the words (1–6) with the photos (A–F). Then listen and check.

| 1 kitchen | 2 bedroom | 3 bathroom |
| 4 living room | 5 dining room | 6 garden |

2 Match the verbs in the list with the rooms in Exercise 1. (Some verbs go with more than one room.)

cook | eat | play football | sleep | wash | watch TV

3 SPEAKING Work in pairs. Have you got the same ideas? What other activities do you do in these rooms?

I talk to my dad in the kitchen.

I sing in the bathroom.

4 SPEAKING Look at the photos on page 49. What can you say about the house?

5 🔊 5.02 Read and listen to the magazine article. Choose the correct option A, B or C.

1 Angelo first went to the cave house because it started to rain.
  A Right B Wrong C Doesn't say
2 Angelo wanted to change the cave house.
  A Right B Wrong C Doesn't say
3 Angelo's parents are Italian.
  A Right B Wrong C Doesn't say
4 Angelo asked a friend to help him paint the house.
  A Right B Wrong C Doesn't say
5 There's no internet in the cave house.
  A Right B Wrong C Doesn't say
6 It's expensive to stay in the cave house.
  A Right B Wrong C Doesn't say

THE 21ST CENTURY CAVEMAN

NO PLACE LIKE HOME | UNIT 5

In 2007, Angelo Mastropietro was in the woods in Worcestershire, UK when it started to rain. He looked for a place to keep dry and he discovered a cave house! The cave house was 800 years old. People lived in the rock-house for hundreds of years, but from about 1962, no one lived there and the house stayed empty.

Angelo liked the rock-house very much. He looked into the possibility of buying it. It was for sale and in 2010 he decided to get it. After that, he started to cut into the rock and to rebuild and modernise the house.

Angelo (who is English, even though his name is Italian) finished the house in nine months. He was a businessman before he started the house, and before 2007 he was quite ill, so he wanted a place where it was possible for him to live in a happy and healthy way. He realised that he didn't need to live in a huge apartment and that being closer to nature could help him feel better.

He worked for over a thousand hours from beginning to end, and he used £160,000 to buy the house and all the things that he needed. He planned everything himself, he moved about 80 tons of rock himself and he painted the house. Angelo tried to make a comfortable place to live. The house has electricity, hot water and wi-fi, and there is heating under the floors of the rooms. Angelo opened a deep hole 80 metres under the house to get natural water.

The house is not huge. It is about 65 m², with one bedroom, a living room, a kitchen and a bathroom with a shower. Angelo doesn't live there all the time, but he uses the house as a place to go to sometimes, to get away from his busy city life. It's also possible to rent the house and to stay there for a weekend or more. This means that other people are able to enjoy Angelo's happy house and maybe escape from their busy lives for a few days, too.

TH!NK values

Following your dreams

6 Look at what some people said about Angelo's project. Find the sentences in the text that support their reasons.

That's too much work for one person.

He needs a lot more money to get everything.

Sometimes it's good to escape from everyday life.

Working a lot is not good for him. Angelo needs to look after his health.

7 **SPEAKING** In pairs imagine you are Angelo. What do you say to the people in Exercise 6?

It's not too much work.

It's fun.

I'm not in a hurry and I feel good when I finish each part of it.

49

GRAMMAR
Past simple (regular verbs)

1 Find the past simple forms of these verbs in the article and write them below. Then complete the rule.

0 start _started_
1 stay _____
2 decide _____
3 finish _____
4 want _____
5 realise _____
6 work _____
7 use _____
8 plan _____
9 try _____

RULE: Use the past simple to talk about finished actions in the past.
With regular verbs:
- We usually add ¹⁰_____ to the verb (e.g., start – started / stay – stayed).
- If the verb ends in -e (e.g., use), we add ¹¹_____ .
- If a short verb ends in consonant + vowel + consonant (e.g. plan), we double the ¹²_____ and add -ed.
- We add -ed to verbs ending in vowel + -y (e.g., stayed).
- If the verb ends in consonant + -y (e.g., try), we change the -y to ¹³_____ and add ¹⁴_____ .

2 Complete the sentences. Use the past simple form of the verbs.

0 I _looked_ (look) up the cave house on the internet. It's amazing.
1 We _____ (start) to paint our house last month and we _____ (finish) yesterday.
2 She _____ (decide) to change her bedroom, so she _____ (paint) the walls blue.
3 We _____ (try) to find another house last year because we _____ (want) to move.
4 I _____ (visit) my aunt and uncle because they _____ (want) to show me their new flat.
5 My parents _____ (study) lots of ideas for a new kitchen before they _____ (order) it.
6 On my last holiday, I _____ (stay) with my grandparents and _____ (help) them tidy up the garden.
7 Last weekend, John _____ (plan) to organise his room, but he _____ (watch) television instead.

→ workbook page 46

PRONUNCIATION
-ed endings /d/, /t/, /ɪd/ Go to page 120.

VOCABULARY
Furniture

3 🔊 5.05 Match the words with the photos. Write 1–12 in the boxes. Then listen and check.

1 armchair | 2 carpet | 3 cooker | 4 curtains
5 desk | 6 lamp | 7 mirror | 8 shelves
9 shower | 10 sofa | 11 toilet | 12 wardrobe

A ☐ G ☐
B ☐ H ☐
C ☐ I ☐
D ☐ J ☐
E ☐ K ☐
F ☐ L ☐

4 SPEAKING Work in pairs. Where are these things in your house? Tell your partner.

> There are mirrors in our bathroom, in my parents' bedroom and in our living room.

→ workbook page 48

NO PLACE LIKE HOME UNIT 5

LISTENING

5 **SPEAKING** Work in pairs. Describe the pictures.

1 _____

2 _____

3 _____

4 _____

6 🔊 5.06 Listen to four people talking about their favourite room. Write the names under the correct pictures.

Andrew | Jo | Paula | Tom

7 🔊 5.06 Listen again. Answer the questions.
1 Who does Jo's favourite room belong to?
2 What does Jo like doing there?
3 Where is the music room?
4 What does Andrew like doing there?
5 Why does Paula like her kitchen?
6 How does she feel there?
7 Where is Tom's favourite room?
8 How long did he stay in it?

GRAMMAR
Modifiers: *quite, very, really*

8 Complete the sentences with *quite*, *very* and *really*. Write the name of the person from Exercise 6 who says them and complete the rule.

1 We sit and talk and I feel _____ relaxed. _____
2 It makes me feel _____ nice and warm. _____
3 It was still _____ dark. _____

> **RULE:** Use words *very*, *really* and *quite* to say more about an adjective.
> The words *very* and ^{4}_____ are used to make an adjective stronger. The word ^{5}_____ usually means 'a little bit'.

9 Write true sentences about your home using the words.

0 kitchen – big / small
   Our kitchen isn't very big / It's quite small.
1 bedroom – tidy / untidy
2 sofa – comfortable / uncomfortable
3 home – busy / quiet

→ workbook page 47

WordWise: Phrasal verbs with *look*

10 Look at these sentences from the unit. Complete them with the words from the list.

after | at | for | into | up

1 Angelo looked _____ the possibility of buying it.
2 I love looking _____ his trains.
3 Angelo needs to look _____ his health.
4 I looked _____ the cave house on the internet.
5 He looked _____ a place to keep dry.

11 Choose the correct word in each dialogue.

1 A What's Janet doing?
   B She's looking *after / like* the baby.
2 A Why are you looking *for / at* me like that?
   B Because I'm angry with you.
3 A I can't find my pen.
   B I'll help you look *after / for* it.
4 A Do the police know what happened?
   B No, they are still looking *for / into* it.
5 A What does this word mean?
   B I don't know. Let's look it *after / up* in the dictionary.

→ workbook page 48

51

Home   New posts   Archives

DAY 6 — Our holiday castle

We're still in Ireland. We arrived in Dublin four days ago. My sister and I liked it a lot – it was great – we weren't bored at all! Then yesterday, after lunch, Dad hired a car and we travelled to the west of Ireland – it didn't take very long, just about two and a half hours, but that was a bit boring. But, after two hours, Dad turned round to us and said: 'We've got a surprise for you. Tonight our hotel is a castle! How exciting is that!' A joke, right? Wrong! We didn't think he was serious, but he was!

At the end of the journey, we stopped outside a real castle. A nice lady welcomed us and started to show us around. What an amazing place! Can you believe that we walked up fifty stone steps to get to the living room?

The castle is over 600 years old, but it had everything we needed. There was a bedroom for our parents and we each had a bedroom, too. But I didn't sleep very well last night – I was so excited to be in a real castle!

This morning we had breakfast and then we climbed up to the top of the castle. We were amazed at the beautiful countryside around us. Then it started to rain and there was a fantastic rainbow – I love rainbows!

The place was so great, we didn't want to leave. This afternoon we want to go to Limerick, so we're packing our bags again! Can it be as good as a castle? Let's see.

> The castle is more than _____ years old.

> There was more than one _____ .

> There were _____ stone steps to climb up!

> In the morning there was a fantastic _____ .

📖 READING

1 🔊 5.07 Read and listen to Tom's blog and complete the sentences with a word or a number.

2 Put the events in order 1–7.
- ☐ Tom finds out where they are staying the night.
- ☐ Tom finds it difficult to sleep.
- ☐ Tom's family leave Dublin.
- ☐ Tom visits the top of the castle.
- ☐ Tom looks around the castle.
- ☐ Tom sees a rainbow.
- ☐ The family get ready to go to Limerick.

✏️ WRITING

3 Use your answers in Exercise 2 to write a summary of the text in no more than 100 words.

Tom really liked Dublin ...

52

NO PLACE LIKE HOME   UNIT 5

Grammar rap! ▶14

Look
We use *-ed* adjectives to say how we feel about something.
We use *-ing* adjectives to say what we think about something or to describe something.

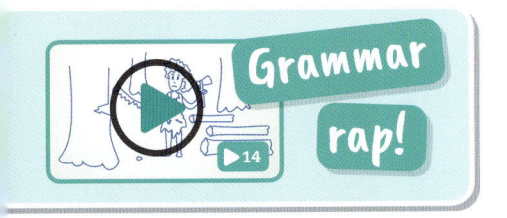

GRAMMAR
Past simple negative

4 **Complete the sentences from Tom's blog and then complete the rule.**

1 We _____ think he was serious.
2 I _____ sleep very well last night.
3 We _____ want to leave.

RULE: To make any verb negative in the past simple, use ⁴_____ + the base form of the verb.

5 **Make Tom's sentences negative.**

0 We talked to local people.
We didn't talk to local people.
1 I enjoyed the car journey.
2 I looked down from the top of the castle.
3 We arrived in Dublin.
4 It rained in the afternoon.

6 **SPEAKING** Work in pairs. Tell your partner two things that you did and two things that you didn't do last weekend. Choose from the verbs in the list.

clean | climb | dance | help | play
study | travel | use | walk | work

→ workbook page 47

VOCABULARY
Adjectives with *-ed* / *-ing*

7 **How is Tom feeling? Write the adjectives under the pictures. One adjective isn't used.**

amazed | annoyed | bored | interested | relaxed

1  _____   3 _____
2  _____   4 _____ 

8 **What did Tom say about Dublin? Complete the sentences with *interested* or *interesting*.**

1 I was really _____ in Dublin.
2 The shops were very _____ .

9 **Choose the correct words.**

1 I get *annoyed / annoying* when people ignore me.
2 His painting was brilliant. I was *amazed / amazing*.
3 Bob talks about football all the time! He's really *bored / boring*.
4 A hot shower is always very *relaxed / relaxing*.
5 I think Maths is really *interested / interesting*.

10 **Complete the sentences so that they are true for you.**

1 I'm never bored when _____ .
2 I find _____ really annoying.
3 _____ is the most amazing singer.
4 I'm really interested in _____ .
5 I'm never relaxed when _____ .

11 **SPEAKING** Work in pairs. Compare your answers.

→ workbook page 48

WRITING
A blog post

12 **PLAN** Think about a real holiday that you went on or an invented holiday. Make notes about these questions.

1 Where did you go? _____
2 Who did you go with? _____
3 What did you do that was very special / different? _____
4 What did you like / not like about the holiday? _____
5 What was *boring / exciting / amazing / interesting / annoying* about the holiday? _____

13 **PRODUCE** Use your notes from Exercise 12 to write a blog post about your holiday. Write about 120–150 words. Write three paragraphs.

Paragraph 1 – your answers to 1 and 2
Paragraph 2 – your answer to 3
Paragraph 3 – your answers to 4 and 5

53

DEVELOPING SPEAKING

1 🔊 5.08 Look at the photo. What is the woman doing? How does she feel? Listen and read to check.

John:	I'm tired. Let's stop now, Mandy. I'm not so sure why we're doing this, to be honest.
Mandy:	You know why, John. We're going to houses to sell these biscuits and the money goes to help homeless people.
John:	I know.
Mandy:	Hang on! This is Mrs Grundy's house. Let's not waste our time here. I don't think she'll give us any money. She's really unfriendly.
John:	I know what you mean. Last week, she shouted at me and Ben because we were 'being noisy' in the street!
Mandy:	Maybe she's just a bit lonely.
John:	I know, but it's not really our problem. Come on.
Mrs Grundy:	Hello! Can I help you?
Mandy:	Um, hello. Well, we're selling biscuits, to help homeless people.
Mrs Grundy:	What a good idea. Can I buy some?
Mandy:	Erm … sure. They're two pounds for a bag.
Mrs Grundy:	OK. Give me two bags. And here's ten pounds. Don't worry about any change, though. Bye!
Mandy:	Wow. So, Mrs Grundy isn't so unfriendly after all. I was completely wrong!
John:	Yes, we were wrong. But it's not a big deal. Anyway, that's ten pounds. We could stop now!
Mandy:	I don't think that's a good idea, John. We've still got six bags to sell. Why don't we do another six houses? Then, how about playing tennis?
John:	Great idea!

2 🔊 5.08 Read and listen again. Correct the wrong information.

1 John and Mandy are selling cakes to get money for homeless people.
2 They think Mrs Grundy is nice.
3 Mrs Grundy buys two bags and pays five pounds.
4 Mrs Grundy wants her change.
5 After Mrs Grundy leaves, they still have ten bags to sell.

3 SPEAKING Work in pairs. Think about the dialogue and answer the questions.

1 What do John and Mandy think about Mrs Grundy? Why do they think this?
2 How are they wrong?

Phrases for fluency

4 Find these expressions in the dialogue. Who says them? Write J (John), M (Mandy) or MG (Mrs Grundy) in the boxes.

1 … not a big deal. ☐
2 …, to be honest. ☐
3 I know what you mean. ☐
4 It's not really our problem. ☐
5 Hang on! ☐
6 …, though. ☐

5 Use the expressions in Exercise 4 to complete the mini-dialogues.

1 A He's usually nice. Today, he's a bit angry, _____ .
   B _____ . He just shouted at me!
2 A You've got to help me with my homework!
   B _____ ! It's your homework – so it's _____ .
3 A It's only a quiz. It's _____ . Right?
   B Well, I'm a bit worried about it, _____ .

⚙ FUNCTIONS
Making and responding to suggestions

KEY LANGUAGE

How about …?	Great idea.
Why don't we …?	I'm not so sure …
Let's …	OK.
We could …	I don't think that's a good idea.

6 Complete the mini-dialogues with one word from the Key Language box.

0 A How *about* playing tennis?
  B Great *idea* .
1 A We _____ do another six houses.
  B I don't think that's a _____ idea.
2 A _____ stop now. I'm tired.
  B OK.
3 A Why _____ we go home now?
  B I'm not so _____ .

ROLE PLAY At a market

Work in pairs. Student A: Go to page 127. Student B: Go to page 128. Take two or three minutes to prepare. Then have a conversation.

LIFE COMPETENCIES

Sometimes it's easy to make judgements about people based on their appearance, but every individual person is different. Making judgements about people ignores their differences. Differences are good because they are what give people their characters.

Be careful making judgements

1 ▶ 15 Watch the video. What does he say about his sister Kate?

2 ▶ 15 Watch again and complete the sentences.
1 He isn't studying. He's reading a _____ .
2 Never judge a _____ by its cover.
3 The man playing guitar isn't _____ . He's a normal man.
4 The new boy at school isn't unfriendly. He's _____ .
5 The kid who says he's great all the time doesn't have such a good _____ .
6 Don't be too _____ to make a judgement.

3 Read and make a list of all the ideas Edna and Arthur have about teenagers.

They don't respect other people.

Edna The problem with teenagers is that they haven't got any respect for other people. I was on the bus today, for example, and some teenagers were annoying everybody by listening to music on their mobile phones. I think it's good for teenagers to like music, but why don't they use headphones? We don't want to listen to their music. We like different music. They simply don't think about other people.

Arthur I think the problem is all the technology. Young people spend all day playing computer games on their own and not outside meeting people. A lot of computer games are about killing people, not helping people or the local community, so young people aren't interested in those things. I understand that young people need technology these days, but reading and writing are also important. My grandson writes me messages saying 'R U OK?', which is terrible. I feel sorry for their teachers.

4 SPEAKING Compare your answers with a partner.

5 SPEAKING Work in pairs. Discuss these questions.
1 Are the items on your list in Exercise 3 true for all teenagers?
2 Do you think Edna and Arthur are right to say all teenagers are like this?
3 Can you think of a teenager who isn't like this? Describe them.
4 Why is it a problem that these old people see teenagers like this?

Me and my world

6 SPEAKING Complete the sentences about someone you made a wrong judgement about. Share your answers with a partner.

Someone I changed my opinion of is _____ .
At first he/she seemed to be _____ .
Now I think he/she is _____ .
I changed my opinion because _____ .

TIPS FOR NOT MAKING JUDGEMENTS

- Don't judge people based on their appearance. Take time to know them better and then form an opinion.
- Don't impose your own values onto others. Find out and try to understand other people's values.
- Avoid generalising about groups of people. Remember groups are made up of individuals with their own personalities and beliefs.

6 FRIENDS FOREVER

OBJECTIVES

FUNCTIONS:
saying what you like doing with others; talking about friends and friendships; talking about past events

GRAMMAR:
past simple (irregular verbs); double genitive; past simple questions

VOCABULARY:
past time expressions; personality adjectives

Get TH!NKING
Watch the video and think: what makes a good friend?

READING

1 **SPEAKING** Look at the photos. Say what the relationship between the people is.

They're best friends.

2 **SPEAKING** Which of the following types of friend do you have?
- A good friend at school
- A good friend outside of school
- A family relative who is a friend
- An animal friend

3 **SPEAKING** Work in pairs. Look at the activities. Which people from Exercise 2 do you like doing these with? What else do you do together?

watch a film | go for a walk | hang out
study | talk about life | go shopping
play sport | do nothing

4 Look at the photos and the title on page 57. What do you think the article is about?

5 **6.01** Read and listen to the web article. Check your ideas.

6 Read the article again. Then correct the information in these sentences.
1 Joe had a problem with his eyes.
2 After the operation, Joe was fine.
3 Joe's mother thought yoga could help Joe.
4 Joe met Fonzie in a hotel swimming pool.
5 Joe gave Fonzie food with his right hand.
6 Joe is now over 30 and still has a lot of problems.
7 Joe's mother opened a centre called Dolphin Plus.
8 Fonzie died when Joe was 12.

56

FRIENDS FOREVER   UNIT 6

A special friendship

This is the story of Joe and Fonzie. It's a story about a friendship that started more than 20 years ago. It's also a story about a friendship that saved a life and started a new kind of help for people with problems.

'Joe' is Joe Hoagland, who was three years old when the story began. And 'Fonzie' is a 3-metre-long, 275 kilogram dolphin.

When Joe was born, he had a problem with his heart and doctors had to operate on him. When he was three, he had another operation. This operation didn't go well and he became paralysed – he couldn't move the left side of his body. The doctors at the hospital didn't think he could get better. Deena, Joe's mother, took him to different places for therapy, but it wasn't very successful. Then the family moved to Florida. Joe liked being in the water and Deena thought swimming could help him. First, they went to swimming pools in hotels, but some hotel guests didn't like them being there. Then one day she went with Joe to a place in Key Largo called Dolphin Plus, where people swam with dolphins. Joe met Fonzie there and the story really began.

Soon, Joe wanted to see Fonzie every day. He loved playing with him and feeding him. Every time that Joe arrived, Fonzie came to see him. Joe's mother told him always to feed Fonzie using his left hand, so Joe used his left side more and more. Slowly, he got better and better. He's now over 30 years old and very well. Deena saw that Joe's friendship with Fonzie helped him a lot, and she knew it was a good idea for other people, too. So, she and her family worked to open a place called Island Dolphin Care. It's next to Dolphin Plus and many people with health problems come to spend time with the dolphins.

Sadly, Fonzie died in 2004 when Joe was 17. He wrote: 'Fonzie was a great friend to me; he and I shared a lot of good times. He always put a smile on my face.'

TH!NK values

Friendship

7   Tick (✓) the boxes that are important for you in a friendship.

A good friend …
- [ ] helps you when you have a problem.
- [ ] makes you laugh when you're sad.
- [ ] never criticises you.
- [ ] is honest with you all the time.
- [ ] looks good.
- [ ] has the same interests as you.

8   **SPEAKING** Put the values from Exercise 7 in order of importance for you. 1 = not important / 6 = very important. Compare your order with a partner.

GRAMMAR
Past simple (irregular verbs)

1 Read these sentences from the article on page 57. All the verbs are in the past simple. How are the verbs in 1 different from the verbs in 2?

1 Then the family **moved** to Florida.
Joe **wanted** to see Fonzie every day.
2 Deena, Joe's mother, **took** him to different places for therapy.
She **knew** it was a good idea for other people, too.

2 Look back at the article on page 57. Write the past simple forms of these verbs.

0 have	_had_	4 think	_____
1 swim	_____	5 come	_____
2 go	_____	6 write	_____
3 see	_____	7 begin	_____

3 Find at least four more irregular past simple forms in the article on page 57. Write the verbs.

4 Correct these two sentences from the article. Make them negative.

1 Joe's operation went well.

2 The doctors thought he could get better.

5 Look at the pictures and the prompts and write the sentences in the past simple.

→ workbook page 54

1 We / go / to Italy but we / go / to Rome
We went to Italy, but we didn't go to Rome.

2 Holly / come / to my party / but Andy / come

VOCABULARY
Past time expressions

6 Complete the lists with the expressions below.

> a year | morning | month

When we talk about the past, we often use expressions like these:
- yesterday, yesterday ¹_____, yesterday afternoon
- last night, last week, last ²_____, last December
- an hour ago, two weeks ago, a month ago, ³_____ ago

7 Complete the sentences with a time expression with *ago*.

0 Oli is twenty. He left school when he was sixteen.
Oli left school four years ago.

1 It's 8 o'clock. I had breakfast at 7 o'clock.
I had breakfast _____

2 It's 10.20. The film began at 10.00.
The film _____

3 It's December. Your holiday was in July.
My holiday _____

8 Complete the sentences with your own information. Use irregular verbs.

1 A year ago, I _____.
2 Ten years ago, I _____.
3 Last year, I _____.
4 Yesterday morning, I _____.
5 Last night, I _____.

→ workbook page 56

3 I / see / James but I / see / Anna

4 I make / sandwiches but I / make / a cake

FRIENDS FOREVER UNIT 6

LISTENING

9 Which sentences do you agree with?
1 A friend never calls you silly.
2 You don't have to be best friends with someone forever.
3 A friend always forgives.

10 🔊 6.02 Listen to Jack talking to his mother. What is the real message of the story?
- ☐ Don't expect friends to always be perfect.
- ☐ A best friend is for life.
- ☐ Your parents were young once, too.

11 🔊 6.02 Listen again and choose the right answer A, B or C.
1 Who doesn't Jack want to invite to his house?
  A Steve
  B Leo
  C Markus
2 Why is Jack upset with Markus?
  A Markus said something mean to him.
  B Markus doesn't want to be his friend anymore.
  C Markus didn't invite him to his house.
3 Who is Janice?
  A a friend of Jack's mum
  B a friend of Jack's
  C a friend of Jack's grandmother
4 How was Janice the next day?
  A really friendly
  B a little bit upset
  C really angry
5 What did Jack's mum feel like doing after she talked to Janice?
  A saying sorry
  B laughing
  C crying
6 What does Jack decide to do at the end of the conversation?
  A wait for Markus to apologise
  B go to Markus' house and talk to him
  C phone Markus and apologise

GRAMMAR
Double genitive

12 Read the sentences. Then choose the correct options to complete the rule.

She's <u>a friend of mine</u>.   Markus is <u>a friend of Jack's</u>.
Her mother was <u>a friend of my mother's</u>.

> **RULE:** We form the 'double genitive' in two ways:
> noun + *of* + possessive ¹***pronoun** / *adjective* (*mine, yours, his, hers, ours, yours, theirs*)
> noun + *of* + possessive ²*pronoun* / ***adjective*** (*my, your, his, her, our, your, their*) + noun/name + possessive *'s*
> We use it to talk about 'one of many things' we have. (e.g., *Lee is one of many friends I have.*)

13 Choose the correct words.
0 She's a friend of *me /* (*mine*).
1 Mr Smith is a teacher of *my sister / my sister's*.
2 She's a cousin of *John / John's*.
3 Mrs Jones is a neighbour of *ours / us*.

14 Rewrite the underlined parts of the sentences.
0 See that man? He's <u>my father's friend</u>.
  He's <u>a friend of my father's</u>.
1 Steve is <u>our friend</u>.
  Steve is _____ .
2 Mike borrowed <u>my shirt</u>.
  Mike borrowed _____ .
3 I lost <u>my mum's book</u>.
  I lost _____ .

→ workbook page 55

Train to TH!NK

Making decisions

15 Draw a spider diagram.
- Write the names of people who are close to you (friends, family).
- What do these people like? Write your ideas.

people close to me

16 🗣 SPEAKING Work in groups. Imagine you had an argument with a friend and want to buy them a small present to say sorry. Show your spider diagrams, make suggestions and decide on a present for each person.

59

READING

1. **Read the magazine article quickly. Complete the sentence.**

   Paul and Annette met in person for the first time _____ .

2. 🔊 **6.03** **Read and listen to the article. Put the events in the order they happened. Two things didn't happen.**

   - [ ] a Paul and Annette met in Singapore.
   - [ ] b Paul and Annette stopped correcting the mistakes in their emails.
   - [ ] c Paul and Annette started writing to each other over the internet.
   - [ ] d Paul asked Annette to marry him.
   - [ ] e Paul and Annette decided to meet.
   - [1] f Annette decided she wanted to get better at English.
   - [ ] g Paul and Annette had an argument.
   - [ ] h Paul and Annette got to know each other better.

3. **SPEAKING** **Work in pairs. Tell the story. Use the ideas in Exercise 2.**

   > *Paul and Annette wrote to each other when they were at school.*

FUNCTIONS
Talking about past events

4. **Think about a time when you made a new friend. Make notes.**
   - Who?
   - Where?
   - When?
   - What happened?

5. **In pairs tell your story.**

   > *I met my friend Al five years ago. I was on holiday in France with my family. We were in a small hotel. Al's family were in the same hotel. We became friends on the first day and spent all the holiday together.*

Life Stories
Pen pals for years

This week, Paul (from Brisbane, Australia) and Annette (from Toulouse, France) tell us about their friendship on different sides of the world.

When and how did your friendship start?

Paul Fifteen years ago! We were both fourteen. My school in Australia and her school in France started a virtual exchange programme for people to write to each other over the internet.

Annette I wanted to improve my English and he wanted to improve his French, so we contacted each other.

Did you become friends immediately?

Annette Not really. I thought he was OK but not special. He made lots of mistakes in his French! Haha.

Paul We corrected each other's mistakes. But I made more than her! She corrected everything, too!

Annette Paul always helped me to improve my English, but you know, after a few months, we stopped worrying about writing in perfect English or French and just wrote to each other and talked about ourselves. I began to see that he was a very nice guy, easy-going and cheerful.

Did you feel the same way, Paul?

Paul Yes, I did. She often made jokes that made me laugh. She's really funny.

Annette And we saw that we had a lot of things in common – books we liked, films we liked, things like that. He's also very intelligent.

So, when did you actually meet face-to-face?

Annette Last year. We met in Singapore.

Paul That's right. We wanted to meet up, but it's a long way and the plane tickets are expensive. So we decided to meet halfway. We had a really great time together for about five days.

Which language did you speak?

Paul Haha! Good question. English, almost all the time. Her English is really good!

Annette He's just being kind! But yes, we had a great time. I think we're going to be friends for life. I hope we can meet up again soon.

FRIENDS FOREVER   UNIT 6

Grammar rap! ▶17

GRAMMAR
Past simple questions

6 Put the words in order to make questions. Check your answers in the article on page 60.
1 speak / language / Which / you / did
2 friends / you / Did / immediately / become
3 meet / did / When / you / actually

7 Complete the questions and answers in the table.

Question	Answer
¹_____ I/you/he/she/we/they enjoy the show?	Yes, I/you/he/she/we/they ³_____ .
	No, I/you/he/she/we/they ⁴_____ (did not).
What time ²_____ I/you/he/she/we/they get home?	I/you/he/she/we/they ⁵_____ home at midnight.

8 Match the questions and answers.
1 Did you have a good weekend?
2 Did you play computer games yesterday?
3 Where did you meet your best friend?
4 Who did you text yesterday?
5 What did you have for dinner last night?

a Yes, I did. I completed four levels.
b At school four years ago.
c We had chicken and chips.
d No, I didn't. It rained all the time.
e My best friend.

9 **SPEAKING** Work in pairs. Ask the questions 1–5 and give your own answers.

→ workbook page 55

VOCABULARY
Personality adjectives

10 Look at the pictures. Read the sentences and write the names under the people.

PRONUNCIATION
Stressed syllables in words Go to page 120.

MY FRIENDS

- **Nick is intelligent.** He knows a lot about everything.
- **Amelia is cheerful.** She's always got a smile on her face.
- **Kai is jealous.** He's not happy when you talk to other friends.
- **Ben is helpful.** He's always ready to help you.
- **Ruby is confident.** She's not scared to talk in public.
- **Liz is generous.** She's always happy to share her things with you.
- **Chloe is easy-going.** She never gets angry about anything.
- **Connor is funny.** He always makes me laugh.

1 _____   2 _____

3 _____   4 _____

5 _____   6 _____   7 _____   8 _____

→ workbook page 56

61

TH!NK
Friends in literature

Culture

1 **SPEAKING** What is your favourite book? Who is your favourite author? Compare your ideas.

2 🔊 6.06 Read and listen to the article and write the names of the books in the gaps.

3 🔊 6.06 Read and listen again and complete the table.

	name of friends	where it is set
The Three Musketeers		
The Jungle Book		
The Lord of the Rings		Middle Earth
My Brilliant Friend		

Friends in literature

Is there anyone who doesn't know about those great friends Harry, Hermione and Ron in the Harry Potter books? J.K. Rowling's stories are world-famous, and part of their success is because of the friendship between those three main characters. But there are many examples of great friends in literature. Let's look at some more.

In 1844, French writer Alexandre Dumas wrote _____. The story is about a young man called D'Artagnan who goes to Paris to join the musketeers (special soldiers who protect the king). He meets Athos, Aramis and Porthos, three friends who are the greatest musketeers in France, and they have many adventures together. They often say: 'One for all and all for one', which shows their strong friendship.

_____ (1894) by Rudyard Kipling is a story about animals who are very like people – some good, some not so good. But there is also Mowgli, a small human boy who grows up in the Indian jungle. Many animals want to find him because he knows how to make fire. Mowgli's great friend and guardian is a bear called Baloo and also a black panther called Bagheera, who help him to escape from the tiger, Shere Khan.

_____ (1937–1949) by J.R.R. Tolkien is a fantasy story about Frodo, who gets a ring from his uncle Bilbo Baggins. Frodo lives in a place called the Shire in Middle Earth and has a friend, Sam. When Frodo leaves the Shire on a long journey with the ring, Sam (as well as some other friends) goes with him. Sam's friendship is very important for Frodo: as he faces many dangerous situations, Sam is always there to help him.

A more modern book is _____ (2011) by Elena Ferrante. It is the first of a series of four novels. The story begins in Naples in the 1950s. Elena and Lila are friends at school, but they have a lot of arguments, too. As they grow up, life takes them away from each other. But when they are both old, things happen that bring them together again.

4 VOCABULARY
There are eight highlighted words in the article. Match the words with these meanings. Write the words.

0 the exciting things that happen to people — *adventures*
1 someone who looks after someone else — _____
2 not safe — _____
3 to get away from danger — _____
4 something that goes well — _____
5 more than one of something (films, books, etc.) — _____
6 when people don't agree — _____
7 the people in a book — _____

SPEAKING

5 Discuss in pairs.
1 Which of these books would you like to read most? Why?
2 What other famous fictional friends can you think of?

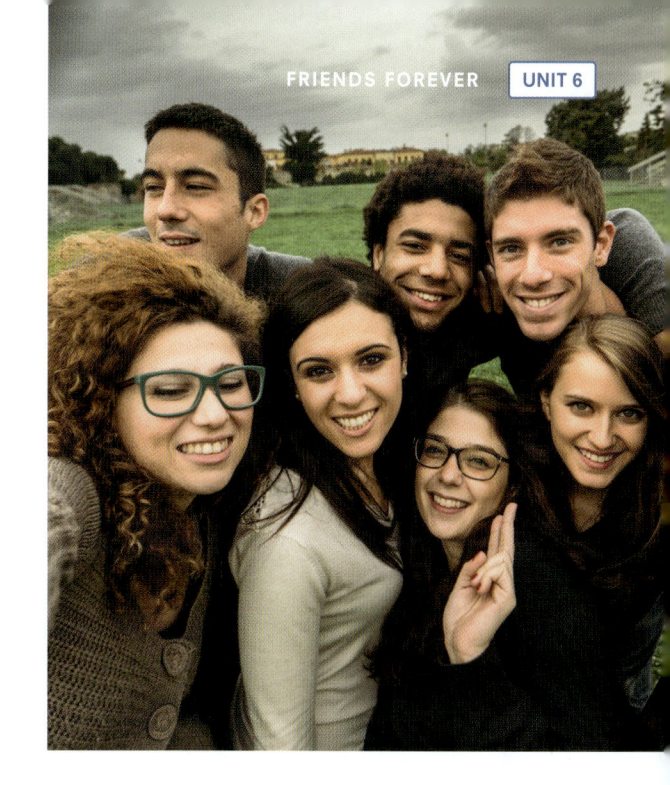

WRITING
A thank you note

1 INPUT Read the message and answer the questions.
1 Why is Liam writing to Darcy?
2 What does he want to do now?

Liam
liamsmith@thinkmail.com

Dear Darcy,
Thank you so much for *The Hunger Games*. You know how much I love reading and I think you found me the perfect book. I finished it last night and it was brilliant. Now I want to read the whole series!
Liam

2 ANALYSE Read the messages. Which is the answer to Liam?

Darcy
darcymiller@thinkmail.com

1 Thanks for your message.
You're welcome. I'm glad you liked it. I thought it was good, too. I've got the next one in the series and you can borrow it if you want. I'll bring it to school on Monday.

Darcy
darcymiller@thinkmail.com

2 Thanks for your message.
I'm sorry I can't come to your birthday party on Friday, but we're going away this weekend. Have a great time.

3 Put the words in the right order to make sentences.
1 book / much / thank / for / the / you / so
2 are / welcome / you
3 it / liked / glad / I'm / you

4 Match the phrases with the photos.
a gift voucher / a box of chocolates / a bunch of flowers

5 Write a sentence for each present.
I ate them all in a day!

6 PRODUCE Imagine you received a present from a friend. Write a thank you note to him/her and say why you liked the present. (60 words)

A2 Key for Schools

READING AND WRITING
Part 1: 3-option multiple choice
→ workbook page 53

1 For each question, choose the correct answer.

1
Room available,
5-bedroom house
£120/month including bills
Shared kitchen and living room
Phone 017896425

A You have your own kitchen and living room in this house.
B Five rooms are now available to rent in this house.
C You don't pay extra for electricity and gas to live in this house.

2
Hi Simon,
Have fun at your piano lesson tomorrow. Shall we go for ice cream afterwards in town? Let me know if you're free then.
Dawn

A Dawn is letting Simon know that she has a music lesson tomorrow.
B Dawn is inviting Simon to do something after his music lesson.
C Simon is telling Dawn he can meet her after the music lesson.

Part 4: 3-option multiple choice cloze
→ workbook page 89

2 Read the article about the White House. Choose the best word (A, B or C) for each space.

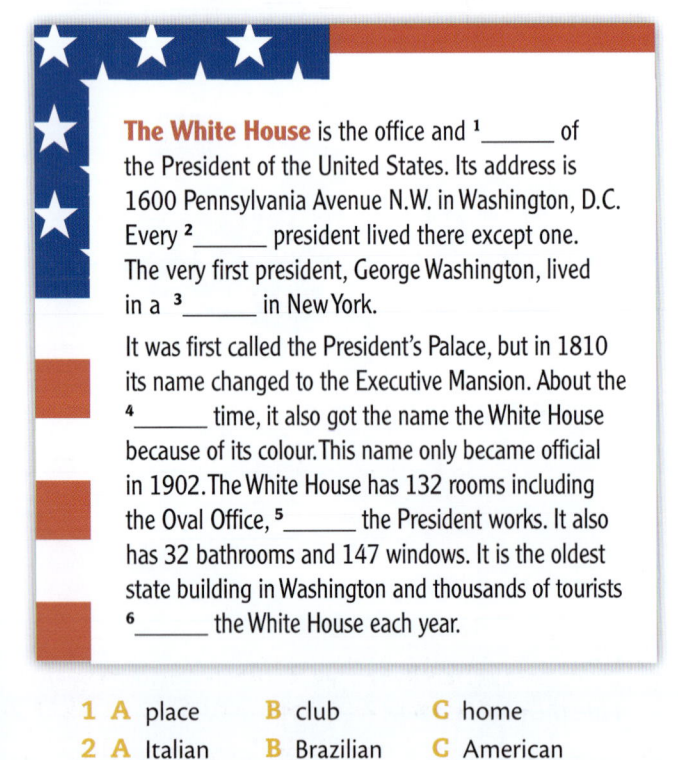

The **White House** is the office and ¹_____ of the President of the United States. Its address is 1600 Pennsylvania Avenue N.W. in Washington, D.C. Every ²_____ president lived there except one. The very first president, George Washington, lived in a ³_____ in New York.

It was first called the President's Palace, but in 1810 its name changed to the Executive Mansion. About the ⁴_____ time, it also got the name the White House because of its colour. This name only became official in 1902. The White House has 132 rooms including the Oval Office, ⁵_____ the President works. It also has 32 bathrooms and 147 windows. It is the oldest state building in Washington and thousands of tourists ⁶_____ the White House each year.

	A	B	C
1	place	club	home
2	Italian	Brazilian	American
3	office	house	shop
4	same	similar	different
5	when	who	where
6	come	go	visit

3
Beginner dance lessons
Wednesdays 5–6.30 pm
£5 pay at the door – no need to book

A You don't need any experience to go to the lessons.
B You need to book a place before you go to the lessons.
C You can try advanced levels of dance on Wednesday.

4
Connor
I forgot to tell you. I'm on holiday in Italy with my parents. I'm afraid I can't go to band practice this week.
Ryan

A Connor would like to know why Ryan wasn't at band practice this week.
B Ryan is telling Connor that he isn't going to any more band practices.
C Ryan is letting Connor know why he can't go to band practice.

5
NEWS
For sale
Kitchen table and four chairs
Only £50
Pick up only

A The furniture is more than £50.
B The furniture is exactly £50.
C The furniture is less than £50.

6
Katie
My friend Emma arrives tomorrow. Come to my house on Friday about 6 pm. I'm having a party to introduce her to my friends.
Trudy

A The party finishes about 6 pm.
B Trudy wants Emma to meet her friends.
C Emma arrives on Friday.

LISTENING
Part 5: Matching
→ workbook page 61

3 🔊 6.07 For each question, choose the correct answer. You will hear Jen talking to Mark about her room. Which piece of furniture did each person give Jen?

Example
0 armchair [C]   C Grandpa

Furniture
1 sofa ☐
2 curtains ☐
3 carpet ☐
4 desk ☐
5 lamp ☐

People
A Dad
B Uncle Tim
C Grandpa
D brother
E Uncle Simon
F Mark
G Mum
H Aunt Abi

64

TEST YOURSELF

UNITS 5 & 6

VOCABULARY

1 Complete the sentences with the words in the list. There are two extra words.

after | annoyed | annoying | cheerful | cooker | do | for | jealous | last | make | really | shower

1 Lucy isn't happy when I see you. I think she's a bit _____ of you.
2 I need to brush my teeth, but Liam is still in the _____ .
3 Dad died when I was 12, so I helped Mum look _____ my little sister.
4 My brother borrowed my tablet and he didn't ask me. I was really _____ .
5 I moved school when I was ten and I found it really difficult to _____ new friends.
6 I'm looking _____ Oliver. Do you know where he is?
7 It's a really _____ song. I really don't like it.
8 I had a great time _____ night – thanks for everything.
9 It's a _____ comfortable bed. I don't want to get up in the mornings.
10 Be careful – the _____ is still hot.

/10

GRAMMAR

2 Complete the sentences with the past form of the verbs in the list.

choose | find | go | like | see | think

1 I _____ he was my friend, but now I'm not so sure.
2 The present was very expensive. I hope she _____ it.
3 I _____ to a party last night and I only got home at 11 pm.
4 I liked the green T-shirt, but eventually I _____ the red one.
5 We _____ a dog all alone in the street, so we took it home.
6 No, not that film. I _____ it last week.

3 Find and correct the mistake in each sentence.

1 I thinked you were at school.
2 Did you enjoyed the film, David?
3 Joy wasn't go to school today. She stayed at home.
4 We were tired so we did go to bed early.
5 Where did you and Connor met?
6 I wasn't hungry, so I didn't ate anything.

/12

FUNCTIONAL LANGUAGE

4 Write the missing words.

1 A How _____ inviting Hugo to our party?
  B I don't think that's a good _____ . Remember the last time he went to a party!
2 A We _____ have pasta for lunch.
  B Let's _____ that. I love pasta!
3 A If you need some money, _____ don't you get a Saturday job?
  B I'm not so _____ . I don't think my dad would like it.
4 A _____ go to town after school.
  B That's a _____ idea. We can go shopping.

/8

MY SCORE /30

22–30 10–21 0–9

65

7 SMART LIFE

OBJECTIVES

FUNCTIONS:
giving advice; talking about obligation / lack of obligation; asking for repetition and clarification

GRAMMAR:
have to / don't have to; should / shouldn't; mustn't vs. don't have to

VOCABULARY:
gadgets; housework; expressions with *like*

Get TH!NKING

Watch the video and think: can you live without your gadgets?

▶ 19

A
B
C
D
E
F

📖 READING

1 🔊 **7.01** Match the words in the list with the photos. Write 1–6 in the boxes. Then listen and check.

1 e-reader	2 digital camera
3 flat screen TV	4 tablet
5 laptop	6 (desktop) computer

2 **SPEAKING** Work in pairs. Talk about the objects.

> I've got a …

> I haven't got a …

> I think the (laptop) in the photo looks (cool / really new / quite old).

3 **SPEAKING** Imagine you could only have one of these things. Which would you choose?

> I'd choose the …
> It's important for me because …
> What about you?

4 🔊 **7.02** Read the sentences and guess the correct answer. Listen and check your answers.

1 A person who **invents** something *has got an idea and creates something new / has got enough money to buy something new.*
2 If you hear something that is **shocking**, it makes you feel *happy and excited / surprised and upset.*
3 I **researched** the topic *on the camera / on the internet.*
4 What is a **huge** problem for Africa? *There is not enough clean water / There is not enough space for people.*
5 You can get **trachoma** from *dirty water / bad food.*
6 Getting an **eye infection** can make people *deaf / blind.*
7 You buy **gel** in a *plastic bottle / paper bag.*

5 **SPEAKING** Work in pairs. Look at the title of the article and the photo on page 67. What do you think the article is about? Compare your ideas with other students.

6 🔊 **7.03** Read and listen to the article about a young inventor. Are the sentences T (true) or F (false)? Correct the false ones.

0 Ludwick Marishane is from South Africa.   T
1 Ludwick used his laptop to find out more about the world's water situation.
2 Thousands of people get trachoma every year.
3 Trachoma is an illness that can make people blind.
4 Ludwick wanted to help people with trachoma.
5 Ludwick's dream was to help people find clean water.
6 DryBath is helping to save a lot of water all over the world.
7 DryBath is a success.
8 Ludwick wants to invent more things.

66

'... just because I didn't want to take a bath'

SMART LIFE — UNIT 7

Ludwick Marishane, a young man from South Africa, was with his friends in Limpopo when they started talking about inventing something to put on your skin so you don't have to take a bath. Ludwick thought that this was a great idea. He used his mobile to do some research on the internet, and he found some shocking facts.

Millions of people around the world haven't got clean water. This is a huge problem because dirty water can create terrible illnesses. One of them is trachoma: thousands of people all over the world get trachoma every year. They wash their faces with dirty water, get an infection and sometimes become blind. To stop trachoma, people don't have to take expensive medication. They don't have to take pills. They don't have to have injections. They have to wash their faces with clean water. That's it.

Ludwick started thinking. He wanted to make something to help people in parts of the world where it's difficult to find clean water. He did more research on his mobile, and he did more thinking. Ludwick had a plan. He wanted to make a gel for people to put on their skin so they don't have to take a bath. He wrote the formula for the gel on his mobile phone. When he was at university, he never stopped thinking about his invention. He started to talk to other people about it, and three years later the dream came true. He made the gel and called it 'DryBath'. It looks like any other gel, but it isn't. This gel saves lives!

Ludwick Marishane is the winner of lots of prizes. People call him 'one of the brightest young men in the world'. He is very happy about his success. DryBath is helping people to be healthy. And DryBath also helps to save water. That's important in many parts of the world where it's difficult to find clean water. Now he wants to invent other things, and he wants to help other young people to become inventors, too.

TH!NK values

Caring for people and the environment

7 Match the values in the list with the sentences in the speech bubbles. Write a–d in the boxes.

a caring about the environment
b caring about the quality of your work
c caring about your appearance
d caring about other people

1 *The water in a lot of rivers and lakes is not clean.*

2 *I need to wash my hair. It's dirty.*

3 *Are you feeling cold? I can give you my jumper.*

4 *Can you switch off the radio, please? I'm doing my homework.*

8 **SPEAKING** Work in pairs. Ask and answer questions about Ludwick Marishane. Try and find as many answers as possible.

*Does he care about the environment?
his appearance?
the quality of his work?
other people?*

He cares about the environment because DryBath helps to save water.

GRAMMAR
have to / don't have to

1 Complete the sentences from the article on page 67 with *have to* and *don't have to*.

1 To stop trachoma, people _____ take expensive medication.
2 They _____ wash their faces with clean water.

2 Complete the rule and the table.

> RULE: Use ¹_____ to say 'this is necessary'.
> Use ²_____ to say 'this isn't necessary'.

Positive	Negative
I/you/we/they ⁰ *have to* help.	I/you/we/they don't have to help.
He/she/it ¹_____ help.	He/she/it ²_____ help.

Questions	Short answers
³_____ I/you/we/they have to help?	Yes, I/you/we/they do. No, I/you/we/they don't.
⁴_____ he/she/it have to help?	Yes, he/she/it ⁵_____ . No, he/she/it ⁶_____ .

3 Match the sentences with the pictures.

1 The bus leaves in 20 minutes. He has to hurry.
2 The bus leaves in 20 minutes. He doesn't have to hurry.

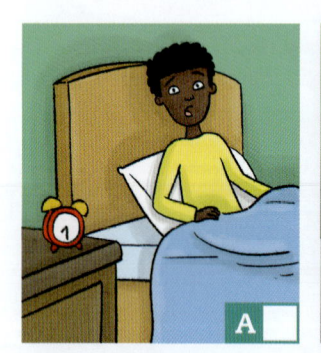

A ☐   B ☐

4 Complete the sentences with *have to / has to* or *don't / doesn't have to*.

1 Our teacher doesn't like mobile phones. We _____ switch them off during lessons.
2 I know that I _____ work hard for this test! You _____ tell me!
3 Ann's ill. She _____ stay home.
4 Your room's a mess! You _____ tidy it up.
5 His English is perfect. He _____ study for exams.
6 I can hear you very well. You _____ shout!

→ workbook page 64

VOCABULARY
Gadgets

5 🔊 7.04 Match the words with the photos. Then listen, check and repeat.

> 1 satnav | 2 MP3 player | 3 torch | 4 games console
> 5 remote control | 6 coffee machine | 7 calculator
> 8 docking station | 9 hair dryer | 10 headphones

A ☐ F ☐
B ☐ G ☐
C ☐ H ☐
D ☐ I ☐
E ☐ J ☐

6 How important are these gadgets for you? Make a list from 1 to 10 (1= most important, 10 = not important at all).

7 SPEAKING Work in pairs. Compare your ideas and tell your partner how often you use these gadgets.

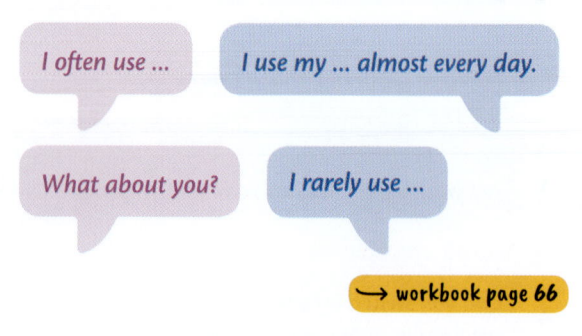

> I often use …
> I use my … almost every day.
> What about you?
> I rarely use …

→ workbook page 66

SMART LIFE UNIT 7

LISTENING

8 **SPEAKING** Look at the pictures of different inventions. Match them with the phrases. Then make sentences to explain what the inventions are. Compare your ideas.

1 not tidy up room / have got robot
2 machine help / ride bike up a hill
3 invention help homework / more time for friends
4 machine can get places around the world / 10 seconds

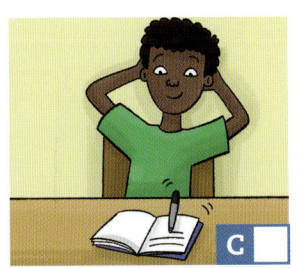

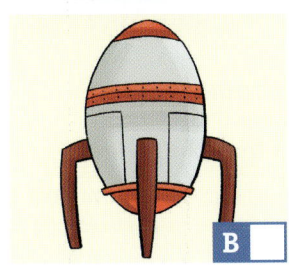

A ☐   C ☐
B ☐   D ☐

The girl in picture A has got a cool machine. It helps her to ride her bike up a hill.

9 🔊 7.05 An expert is talking to a group of teenagers about becoming an inventor. Match the sentence halves to find out what the person says. Then listen and check.

1 Many people think that you have to be older ☐
2 The point is that he invented something ☐
3 It's not a good idea ☐
4 After leaving school, you should ☐

a to make people's lives easier.
b to become an inventor.
c get a job first before trying to become an inventor.
d to work on more than one invention at a time.

10 🔊 7.05 Complete the expert's answers with *should* or *shouldn't*. Listen again and check.

1 You _____ start with an idea to help other people.
2 You _____ think 'How can I get rich?'
3 You _____ only talk to people that you can trust about your ideas.
4 You _____ work on all the ideas at the same time.
5 You _____ get a job and invent things as a hobby.
6 You _____ make sure that you've got a job.

GRAMMAR
should / shouldn't

11 Look at the sentences in Exercise 10. Match the sentence halves.

RULE:
1 Use *should* to say   a 'It's not a good idea.'
2 Use *shouldn't* to say   b 'It's a good idea.'

12 Use *should / shouldn't* and a word from each list to give advice to these people.

~~take~~ | go to | eat | drink | read

~~medicine~~ | book anymore | bed
any more cake | some water

0 I've got a headache. *You should take some medicine.*
1 I'm really thirsty. _____
2 My eyes are tired. _____
3 I'm tired. _____
4 I feel sick. _____

→ workbook page 64

WordWise: Expressions with *like*

13 Match the sentences.

1 This chicken isn't very good. ☐
2 Someone's talking. Who is it? ☐
3 Let's buy her a present. ☐
4 He's a really nice guy. ☐
5 What's that animal? ☐

a Like what? A poster perhaps?
b Yes, he's just like his sister, she's nice, too.
c I'm not sure. It looks like a rabbit, but it isn't.
d That's right. It tastes like fish!
e It sounds like Jim.

14 Complete the dialogues using a phrase with *like*.

1 A I forgot my homework.
   B I'm _____. Mine's at home, too.
2 A Here's a photo of my sister.
   B Wow. She really _____ you!
3 A We should do some exercise.
   B _____? Go for a walk?
4 A Let's go to the cinema.
   B That _____ a great idea.

→ workbook page 66

69

READING

1 **SPEAKING** Work in pairs. Look at the pictures and think about what the machines do. Then choose one of the two machines and talk about it.

> I think it's called …   It helps with …
> It's a cool machine because …

2 🔊 7.06 Read and listen to these product reviews on a website from the year 2066. What do the machines do?

Are you tired of choosing a cool outfit to wear for special occasions? Well, now you don't have to!

The all-new Trendy-wise is easy to use and you don't have to be trendy to use it. However, before you can use it, you have to take photos of all the clothes in your wardrobe. And you mustn't forget to take photos of all your shoes and socks, too. Then all you have to do is click on a photo of, for example, a blue T-shirt. The Trendy-wise selects photos of trousers or skirts, shoes, socks, etc., from your wardrobe to go with this T-shirt. Each time it creates a different outfit for you and the outfits are all very trendy. Oh, I almost forgot! You also have to type in the kind of event/occasion, for example: a concert or a birthday party.

Do you sometimes have bad dreams? Do you wake up scared or unhappy? Yes? Then you should buy the DreamCatcher.

This is how it works: Put the machine on your head before you go to bed. Tell it what you want or don't want by speaking into the microphone – for example: 'I want dreams where I win a singing competition' or 'I don't want dreams about falling.' When you are asleep, DreamCatcher will follow your dreams and make sure you get what you want. Imagine that in your dream you do something dangerous. DreamCatcher will make sure you're safe. Here's an example. Let's say you start to climb a high mountain. You don't have to worry because the DreamCatcher will make you walk back down again.
But you mustn't use the machine every night. It will only work every three days.

---

3 Read the reviews again and answer the questions.
1 What do you have to do before you can use the Trendy-wise?
2 What mustn't you forget to do?
3 What other thing do you have to do?
4 How does the DreamCatcher work?
5 Let's say you have a dangerous dream. How does the DreamCatcher help you?
6 What mustn't you do when you use the DreamCatcher?

Grammar rap! ▶20

GRAMMAR
mustn't / don't have to

4 Complete the sentences from the reviews.
1 You _____ be trendy to use the new Trendy-wise.
2 You _____ forget to take photos of all your shoes and socks, too.

5 Complete the rule with *mustn't* or *don't have to*.

> RULE: Use ¹_____ to say 'it's not necessary'.
> Use ²_____ to say 'don't do it! I'm telling you not to!'

6 Match sentences (1–2) with (a–b).
1 You don't have to go swimming.
2 You mustn't go swimming.

a There are sharks.
b You can do something else if you prefer.

7 Complete the sentences with *mustn't* or *don't have to*.
1 A The film starts soon. We _____ be late.
  B Don't worry. I'm ready now.
2 A I'm so thirsty.
  B Stop! You _____ drink that!
3 A I'm sorry I can't join you.
  B That's fine. You _____ come.
4 A Sorry, I can't stay. I'm in a hurry.
  B No problem. You _____ wait for me.
5 A I can't swim very well.
  B Then you really _____ swim here. The water's deep.

→ workbook page 65

PRONUNCIATION
Vowel sounds: /ʊ/ and /uː/   Go to page 121. 🎧

SMART LIFE UNIT 7

VOCABULARY
Housework

8 🔊 7.09 Match the words with the photos. Write 1–10 in the boxes. Listen and check. Then listen again and repeat.

> 1 vacuum the floor | 2 tidy up | 3 do the ironing
> 4 do the shopping | 5 set / clear the table
> 6 do the washing-up (wash up) | 7 make the beds
> 8 do the cooking | 9 do the washing
> 10 load / empty the dishwasher

→ workbook page 66

SPEAKING

9 Read the questions. Make notes.
1 What do you have to do at home: tidying, shopping, cooking, etc.?
2 What don't you have to do?
3 What should parents / children do at home?

10 Plan what you are going to say. Use these phrases.

> I have to … I think / don't think that's fair.

> I don't have to … I'm quite happy about that.

> But it would be OK for me to do that.

> I think … should do the same amount of work.
> It's not fair that …
> Mothers / Fathers should do more work because …

11 Work in pairs or small groups. Compare your ideas about housework.

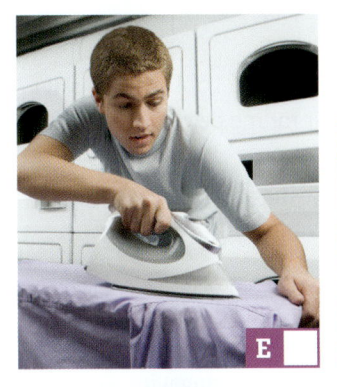

WRITING
A paragraph about housework

12 Ask your partner these questions and make notes. Then write a paragraph.
1 What do you have to do at home?
2 What don't you have to do at home?
3 When do you have to do housework?
4 What do you feel about this housework?

Kate hates clearing the table, but she has to do it every evening. She also has to vacuum her bedroom floor once a week. She doesn't have to do …

71

DEVELOPING SPEAKING

1 🔊 **7.10** Look at the photo. What is the woman looking at? Why is she upset? Listen and read to check.

Ryan: All right, Mum?
Mum: No, not really, Ryan, I really need you to help me.
Ryan: Sorry, Mum? What did you say?
Mum: I said I need some help, Ryan. There are so many things to do in this house.
Ryan: Like what?
Mum: Well, this washing up, for a start. Look at all this! It's terrible. So, can you do it for me before you go out, please?
Ryan: No chance, Mum! I'm leaving soon and I've got lots of things to do. I'm really busy, you know.
Mum: What do you mean?
Ryan: Well, homework and stuff. You know.
Mum: OK. Never mind. You don't have to help me. But I have to leave soon. I have a meeting with a new client. I mustn't be late.
Ryan: Oh, OK. Sorry, Mum. Don't worry. I can do it. Leave it all to me, OK?
Mum: Are you sure?
Ryan: Absolutely. You go now and leave everything to me.
Mum: OK, thanks Ryan. You're a good boy! Bye!
Ryan: OK, well it *is* a lot of washing up, and perhaps I should clean the kitchen, too. But the game starts right now and there's no TV in here. Hmm. Problem. Some creative thinking is needed. Well, it's easy of course. Get my phone. Do live streaming of the game. Put the phone next to the sink. And great! Off we go. And the game's starting. Come on United. Argh, no! That's my new phone!

2 🔊 **7.10** Read and listen again to the dialogue and answer the questions.
1. How do you think Ryan's mum is feeling at the start of the dialogue?
2. Why can't Ryan hear his mum?
3. Why doesn't Ryan want to help his mum?
4. Where do you think Ryan should put his phone?

Phrases for fluency

3 Find the expressions 1–5 in the story. Who says them? How do you say them in your language?

0 No chance.   _Ryan_   3 Absolutely.   _____
1 … and stuff.   _____   4 So, … ?   _____
2 Never mind.   _____   5 All right … ?   _____

4 Complete the dialogue with the expressions in Exercise 3.

A ¹_____, Dan? Do you want to come round tonight? We can play computer games ²_____.
B ³_____. I love computer games, they're awesome!
A Can you bring your new laptop?
B ⁴_____. It's my brother's. I can't take it.
A ⁵_____. We can use mine.
B ⁶_____, is seven o'clock OK?

⚙️ FUNCTIONS
Asking for repetition and clarification

> **KEY LANGUAGE**
> What do you mean?   Sorry?   Like what?

5 Write the expressions from the Key Language box next to their definitions.
a Say that again. _____
b What are you trying to say? _____
c Give me an example. _____

6 Complete the extracts from the conversations with the words from Exercise 5.

Mum Ryan, I really need you to help me.
Ryan ¹_____, Mum? What did you say?
Mum There are so many things to do in this house.
Ryan ²_____?
Ryan I'm really busy, you know.
Mum ³_____?

🎭 ROLE PLAY A phone call

Work in pairs. Student A: Go to page 127. Student B: Go to page 128. Take two or three minutes to prepare. Then have a conversation.

SMART LIFE UNIT 7

LIFE COMPETENCIES

Everybody has problems to solve. Sometimes the problems are big, and sometimes they are small, but it's always a good idea to think of all the possibilities before we decide what to do.

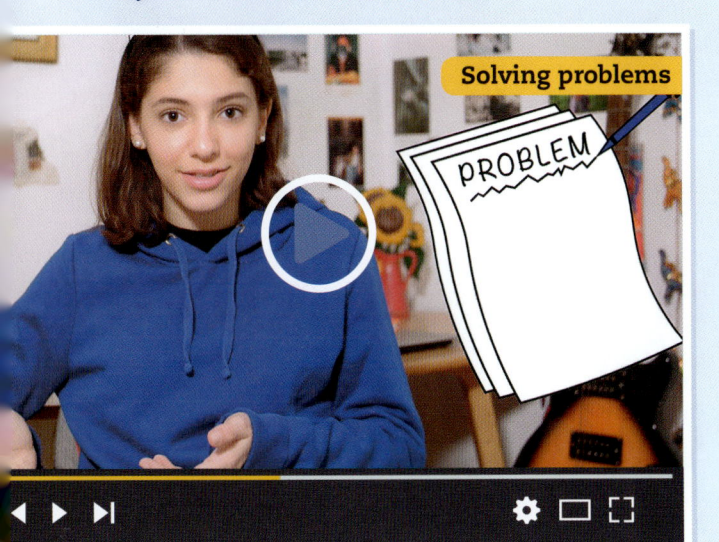

Solving problems

1 ▶21 Watch the vlog and complete the sentence.

'Someone once said that life is just a series of _____ looking for _____.'

Do you think the sentence is true? Why is problem solving important?

2 ▶21 Watch again and complete the notes.

What to vlog about?

1 – Topic: Empathy

For	Against
2 – It's interesting	5 – _____
3 – _____	
4 – _____	

6 – Topic: _____

For	Against
7 – _____	9 – Not really 'Life Lessons'
8 – _____	

TIPS FOR SOLVING PROBLEMS

- When you have a problem, spend some time trying to think of all the possible solutions.
- When you have all the possible solutions, think about the positives and negatives for each solution.
- After listing the positives and negatives, choose what you think the best solution is.
- Remember sometimes there is no good solution and you have to choose the one that is least bad.

3 Read the conversation. What is Ben's problem?

Andy Hey, Ben. What are you doing?

Ben Hello, Andy. I'm thinking about how to go to school next week.

Andy Why?

Ben My mum's car isn't working, so we have to find another way. One idea is getting the bus.

Andy Good idea. The bus is fast, so you can get to school early. So, can we go out now?

Ben Hang on! I can see here that the bus goes at 7.10, so I have to get up at … 6. No chance! Also, I need to take my little sister to her school and I don't want to be at school an hour early.

Andy So why don't you walk? You can take Annie to school, walk from there to my house and then we can go to school together.

Ben Sounds good, but I'm not so sure. Annie's school is a long way from your house. And I don't want to arrive at school late, but I can't leave Annie at her school at 8 am. It's not open until 8.15.

Andy OK, so the bus is a no, and walking a no, too? How about going on your bikes? You can cycle with Annie to her school at 8.15 and have time to get to school about 10 minutes early.

Ben Good idea! But Annie hasn't got a bike.

4 Ben and Andy think of three solutions. What are they? What are the positives and the negatives about each solution?

5 SPEAKING With your partner, think of another solution to Ben's problem. What are the positives and negatives about your solution?

6 SPEAKING Explain your solution to the rest of the class. Who has the best solution?

Me and my world

7 Answer the questions.

a Think of a small, medium and large problem that you have.

b Who can you talk to about these problems?

c Have you got ideas about how to solve them?

73

8 A QUESTION OF SPORT

OBJECTIVES

FUNCTIONS:
talking about sports; talking about feelings; talking about ongoing past events, sequencing events

GRAMMAR:
past continuous; past continuous vs. past simple; *when* and *while*

VOCABULARY:
sport and sports verbs; adverbs of sequence

Get TH!NKING

Watch the video and think: what can you learn from winning and losing?

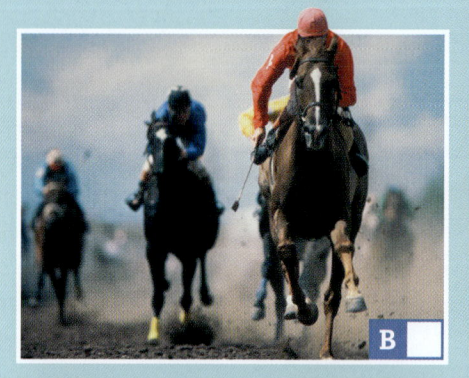

A B C

D E F

READING

1 Match the words in the list with the photos. Write 1–6 in the boxes.

> 1 basketball | 2 horse racing | 3 gymnastics
> 4 athletics | 5 swimming | 6 tennis

2 Which sport(s) in Exercise 1 has these things?

> a ball | a race | a track | water
> bars | a net | a match | a rider

3 Name other sports in English.

4 Which sports are popular in your country? Which ones do you like? Write P (popular) and/or L (like) next to each photo.

5 SPEAKING Compare your ideas with a partner.

> Basketball is popular here, but I don't like it very much.

> I like tennis and it's very popular here.

6 Look at the photos on page 75. Which sports are the stories about?

7 🔊 8.01 Read and listen to the article and check your answers.

8 Read the article again. Are the sentences T (true) or F (false)? Correct the false ones.

1 Usain Bolt won both the 100m and 200m gold medals at three Olympic Games.
2 Bolt won all his gold medals running on his own.
3 Bolt was world champion 11 times.
4 Nadia Comaneci was 16 years old when she got the perfect score.
5 The scoreboard didn't show Comaneci's score correctly.
6 Comaneci scored 10.00 six times at the Montreal Olympics.
7 Some people thought it was impossible to run a mile in four minutes.
8 Roger Bannister did not win a medal at the 1952 Olympic Games.

74

A QUESTION OF SPORT UNIT 8

THE WORLD'S GREATEST SPORTING ACHIEVEMENTS

The world of sport is full of wonderful moments. Here are our top three.

★ The triple double

The starting gun went off. Suddenly, eight athletes were flying down the track in Rio de Janeiro's Olympic Stadium. Less than 20 seconds later the race was over. Usain Bolt was walking around the stadium with the Jamaican flag over his shoulders – he was a double Olympic champion … again! Four years earlier, at the 2012 London Olympics, he became the first man to win a gold medal in both the 100m and 200m sprint at a second Olympic Games (he won them both at the 2008 Beijing Olympics, too). In Rio, he did it for a third time. As well as his eight Olympic gold medals (he won the other two in relay races with other teammates), Bolt also won 11 world championships and currently holds the world record for the 100m and 200m. He is one of the greatest sprinters in history.

★ The perfect ten

Everyone was looking at 15-year-old Romanian gymnast Nadia Comaneci as she left the bars, flew through the air and landed perfectly on the ground. She turned round. The crowd was cheering. Everyone was waiting nervously for the judges' score. Then it came. The scoreboard was showing '1.00'. The crowd was confused. But then the organisers explained. The makers of the scoreboards thought it was impossible to get a perfect score of 10. The boards were not able to show '10.00'. So, on 18 July 1976, at the Montreal Olympics, Nadia made history when she became the first gymnast ever to get a perfect ten. She got six more 'perfect scores' at the games and won three gold medals, making her one of the best athletes in her sport of all time.

★ The four-minute mile

It was the final lap. Roger Bannister was running fast, but could he really become the first person to run a mile in under four minutes? A minute later, he was lying exhausted on the ground. Then, there was an announcement of his time: '3 minutes, 59.4 seconds.' The crowd went crazy.

Before 6 May 1954, experts said that a four-minute mile was impossible to run. Roger showed them that they were wrong. He planned to stop running after the 1952 Summer Olympics, but there he only came in fourth place. Without a medal, Roger wanted to show how good he was. In 1954, he did exactly that.

TH!NK values

Trying, winning and losing

9 Think about these sentences. Which do you agree with most?

1 When you play sport, you should always try your hardest.
2 Having fun is more important than winning.
3 No one remembers the person who finishes second.
4 Getting physical exercise is more important than winning trophies.
5 Sport is the most important thing in life.

10 SPEAKING Work in pairs. Compare your ideas with a partner.

I agree with number 1 the most. What about you?

75

GRAMMAR
Past continuous

1 Complete the sentences from the article on page 75 with the words in the correct form. Then choose the correct words to complete the rule.

cheer | fly | lie | run

1 Eight athletes _____ down the track.
2 The crowd _____ .
3 Roger Bannister _____ fast.
4 A minute later, he _____ exhausted on the ground.

RULE: Use the past continuous to talk about ⁵*completed actions* / *actions in progress* at a certain time in the past.

2 Find more examples of the past continuous in the article on page 75. Then complete the table.

Positive	Negative
I/he/she/it ¹_____ working.	I/he/she/it ³_____ (was not) working.
You/we/they ²_____ working.	You/we/they weren't (were not) working.

Questions	Short answers
⁴_____ I/he/she/it working?	Yes, I/he/she/ it ⁶_____ . No, I/he/she/it ⁷_____ (was not).
⁵_____ you/we/they working?	Yes, you/we/they/ ⁸_____ . No, you/we/they ⁹_____ (were not).

PRONUNCIATION
Strong and weak forms of *was* and *were*
Go to page 121.

3 Yesterday the sports teacher was late. What were the students doing when he got there? Complete the sentences with the correct form of the verbs.

0 Lucy _was talking_ (talk) on her phone.
1 Daniel and Sophie _____ (play) basketball.
2 Samuel _____ (read) a book.
3 Ken and Sarah _____ (climb) up the ropes.
4 Lisa _____ (not think) about sports. She _____ (dream) about a day on the beach.
5 Andy and Matt _____ (not do) any sports. They _____ (look) at photos on Andy's tablet.

4 Complete the dialogues with the past continuous form of the verbs.

1 A What _____ (you/do) yesterday when we phoned you?
  B I _____ (wait) for my mum in town. And it was horrible because it _____ (rain)!
2 A Why didn't you answer when I phoned you?
  B I _____ (cook) my lunch.
3 A Was it a good game yesterday?
  B Well, the beginning was fine. We _____ (play) well and we _____ (win). But then they scored four goals!
4 A _____ (you/watch) TV when I called last night?
  B No, I wasn't. I _____ (read) a magazine.

→ workbook page 72

A F
B G
C H
D I
E J

VOCABULARY
Sport and sports verbs

5 Match the words in the list with the photos. Write 1–10 in the boxes.

1 sailing | 2 diving | 3 golf | 4 gymnastics
5 rock climbing | 6 rugby | 7 snowboarding
8 skiing | 9 volleyball | 10 windsurfing

76

6 Answer the questions.

1 Two of the sports in Exercise 5 have *players* and a *team*. Which ones are they?
2 Seven of the sports in Exercise 5 add *-er* or *-or* for the people who do them. Which ones are they?
3 What do we call someone who does gymnastics?

7 We use different verbs for different kinds of sports. Read the rule and then complete the table with the sports in Exercise 5.

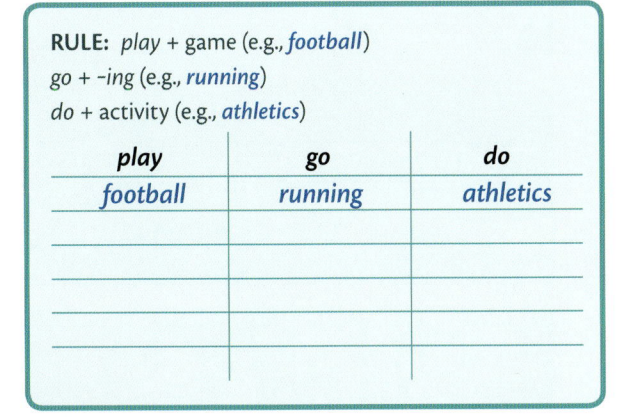

> RULE: play + game (e.g., *football*)
> go + -ing (e.g., *running*)
> do + activity (e.g., *athletics*)

play	go	do
football	running	athletics

8 **SPEAKING** Work in groups. Answer the questions about the sports in Exercise 5.

Which sports …
1 are team sports?
2 are dangerous?
3 are water sports?
4 are in the Winter Olympics?
5 are expensive?
6 are difficult to play or do?

→ workbook page 74

LISTENING

9 🔊 8.04 Five teenagers were asked the question: 'How do you feel about sport?' Listen and draw the correct emoji for each sport they mention.

They really like it. 😊	It's OK for them. 😐	They don't like it. 😒

	Gemma	Andy	Tracey	Paul	Ryan
football					
swimming					
running					
skateboarding					
gymnastics					
skiing					
tennis					

10 🔊 8.04 Listen again. Who expresses these ideas? Write the name.

1 I practise a lot.
___
2 I am not competitive.
___
3 I like doing things alone.
___
4 I'm learning another sport.
___
5 I can't do my sport at school.
___

11 **SPEAKING** Work in pairs. Which of the five teenagers are you like? Tell your partner.

I'm like Ryan. I love all sports.

I'm like Andy because I prefer individual sports.

Look 👁

You can use *like* to say that you have similar interests to somebody or that you have the same abilities.
Sarah's **like** Greg. She loves tennis.
Matt's **like** his brother. They're both good at gymnastics.

FUNCTIONS
Talking about feelings

12 You are going to answer the question: 'How do you feel about sport?' List some sports you want to talk about.

running, football, swimming, surfing

13 What do you want to say about each sport? Mark them ✓ for positive comments; and ✗ for negative ones.

running ✗   football ✗   swimming ✓   surfing ✓

14 Think about why you put ✓ or ✗. Look at the words and ideas in Exercise 8. Use these words and / or other words you know.

running ✗ boring   football ✗ team sport
swimming ✓ fun   surfing ✓ difficult and fun

15 Work in pairs. Ask each other: 'How do you feel about sport?'

How do you feel about sport?

Well, I don't like running because it's boring. But swimming is fun and I love surfing because it's fun and it's difficult to do.

| Home | About | Latest posts | Archive |

Sporting fails 👎

Professional athletes need their bodies to be in excellent condition. They train hours every day to achieve this. Sometimes it only takes one small mistake to spoil all that hard work. In 2011, for example, French golfer Thomas Levet won the French Open. He was so happy that he jumped in a lake and broke his leg. And American skier Lindsey Vonn cut her hand badly while she was opening a glass bottle to celebrate winning at the 2009 World Championships.

We know you're not professionals, but we want you to tell us all about your silliest sporting accidents.

1 Last year, I was playing volleyball for my school team. I jumped up high and hit the ball really hard. At first, I thought it was a really good shot, but I soon found out it wasn't. The ball hit the post at the side of the net: then it hit me in the face and knocked me to the floor. I had a big purple bruise on my face and I couldn't play the rest of the game. *Liam*

2 When I was 13, I played for the school rugby team and we won the schools championship. A few days later, there was a big celebration. All the students were there to watch as we walked on to the stage to get medals from the headmistress. I got my medal, but when I was leaving the stage, I tripped and fell down the steps. Luckily, I wasn't hurt, but I was really, really embarrassed. *Connor*

3 A few days ago I was skateboarding down my road when I saw my best friend. I shouted to him and started waving. While I was waving, I rode into a lamppost and fell off. My leg was hurting really badly and I couldn't move. After ten minutes, my friend called an ambulance. Finally, they took me to hospital. The doctor there told me my leg was broken. Now I can't skateboard for at least six months, and I have to miss the local championships. *Eve*

A

B

C

📖 READING

1 Look at the pictures. What do you think is happening in each one?

2 🔊 8.05 Read and listen to the stories and match them with the pictures. Write the numbers 1–3 in the boxes.

3 Read the forum again. Answer the questions.
  1 Why did the golfer jump into a lake?
  2 How did the skier cut her hand?
  3 After Liam hit the ball, what did it do?
  4 What was Connor doing when he fell?
  5 Why can't Eve skateboard for the next six months?

4 **SPEAKING** How funny do you think these stories are? Give each one a number from 0–5 (0 = not funny at all, 5 = very, very funny). Compare your ideas with a partner.

Train to TH!NK

Sequencing

5 Look at the lists. Put them in a logical order.
  1 morning – night – afternoon – evening
  2 tomorrow – today – next week – yesterday
  3 Saturday – Wednesday – Monday – Friday
  4 have lunch – come home – go to school – wake up
  5 baby – adult – child – teenager
  6 first half – kick-off – half-time – second half

6 **SPEAKING** Compare your ideas with other students. Are they the same or different?

A QUESTION OF SPORT   UNIT 8

Grammar rap! ▶23

GRAMMAR
Past continuous vs. past simple

7 Look at these sentences from the stories on page 78. Which verbs are in the past continuous and which verbs are in the past simple?

1 Lindsey Vonn cut her hand badly while she was opening a glass bottle.
2 When I was leaving the stage, I tripped and fell down the steps.
3 I was skateboarding down my road when I saw my best friend.
4 While I was waving, I rode into a lamppost.

8 Look at the diagram. Which part tells us the background action? Which part says what happened at one moment? Complete the rule.

I was skateboarding down the road.

I saw my best friend.

RULE: Use the ¹_____ to talk about background actions in the past, and the ² _____ for actions which happened at one moment (and sometimes interrupted the background action).

9 Complete the sentences. Use the past continuous or past simple form of the verbs.

0 He __was running__ (run) and he suddenly __felt__ (feel) a pain in his leg.
1 The ball _____ (hit) me while I _____ (watch) a bird.
2 Jenny _____ (sail) with her father when she _____ (see) some dolphins.
3 He _____ (chase) the ball and he _____ (fall) over.
4 When I _____ (look) out of the window, it _____ (snow).

when and while

10 Look at Exercise 9. Complete the rule.

RULE: We often use *when* before the past ¹_____ and *while* before the past ² _____ .

11 Complete the sentences with the correct form of the verbs. Use past continuous for the longer activity and past simple for the shorter one.

| arrive | go | have (x2) | ~~ring~~ |
| see | talk | walk | watch | ~~write~~ |

0 I _____was writing_____ an email. My phone _____rang_____ .
1 Alex and Sue _____ a film. Their friends _____ .
2 Marco _____ breakfast. He _____ a great idea.
3 Cristina _____ on the phone. Her father _____ out.
4 They _____ in the mountains. They _____ a strange bird.

12 Join the sentences in Exercise 11 in two different ways. Use *when* and *while*.

→ workbook page 73

VOCABULARY
Adverbs of sequence

13 Match the parts of the sentences.

1 At first,   a 15 minutes, they phoned 999.
2 Then   b they took me to hospital.
3 After   c I thought it was a really good shot.
4 Finally,   d it came straight back towards me.

14 Complete the story with the words in Exercise 13.

¹_____ , I was very nervous.
²_____ the starter fired the gun.
³_____ ten seconds, I crossed the finish line and won! I was the world champion!
⁴_____ the photographers took photos of me.  
⁵_____ an hour, they gave me the gold medal.
⁶_____ , I woke up.

→ workbook page 74

79

Culture

TH!NK The wonderful world of sport

1. Look at the photos and answer the question. Then say what you think the article is about. Where can you see the following things?
   - people climbing
   - a net
   - camels
   - a chess board

2. 🔊 8.06 Read and listen to the article. Match the pictures with the sports (1–4).

3. **SPEAKING** Which sport do you like most? Which do you not like? Compare your ideas with others in the class.

The wonderful World of sport

Sports such as football, tennis and golf are popular all over the world with millions of people playing them or watching them on TV. But there are also many unusual sports that are not so well known. Here are four interesting examples.

1 Every year, on a small Chinese island, thousands of people arrive to celebrate a very special event: the Cheung Chau bun festival. The highlight of the festival is a race to the top of a very strange mountain. The mountain is made of metal and covered with a type of traditional Chinese bun. Spectators watch as three teams compete to see how many buns they can take from the mountain. The climb can be quite dangerous and people who want to take part must take a special training course.

2 Camel racing is a popular sport in many countries around the world, including Mongolia and Australia. But it is especially popular in the Middle East and each year, from late October to early April, many big races take place in countries such as the United Arab Emirates. As many as 70 camels race along sandy desert tracks for up to 16 km. The owners of the camels drive by the side of the animals shouting at them to run faster and cross the finish line before the others.

3 Bossaball is a very modern sport that was first played in 2005. It started in Spain, but it was the idea of a Belgian man called Filip Eyckmans. He wanted to create a sport that mixed together football, gymnastics, volleyball and the Brazilian music of bossa nova. There are two trampolines with a net between them. The idea is for one team to hit the ball over the net and the other team to try and hit it back. The trampolines let the players jump very high, making the sport very exciting to watch. The sport is already popular in many countries around the world, including Brazil, Mexico, Turkey, Singapore and Saudi Arabia.

4 Chess boxing was the invention of Dutch artist Iepe Rubingh. His original idea was to create a piece of performance art, but it was so popular that it soon became a sport played in countries all over the world. The game is quite simple. Two contestants compete against each other at chess and boxing. Each round of chess is followed by a round of boxing with a break of a minute between each round to give the players time to put on or take off their gloves. The first person to win either the chess match or the boxing match wins the game.

4 Read the article again and answer the questions. Why …

1 do thousands of people go to a Chinese island every year?
2 do people climb the metal mountain?
3 do camel owners drive beside the camels and shout?
4 did Filip Eyckmans create bossaball?
5 is bossaball exciting to watch?
6 do people playing chess boxing stop for one minute?

5 VOCABULARY There are eight highlighted words in the article. Match the words with these meanings. Write the words.

0	are involved in an activity or sport	*take part*
1	the people who try to win a race / game / quiz (etc.)	_____
2	a short time between two things	_____
3	happen	_____
4	a competition to see who is the fastest at something	_____
5	people who watch a race or game	_____
6	to go across from one side of something to another	_____
7	a small, sweet cake (usually round)	_____

WRITING
An article about a sporting event

1 INPUT Read Joanna's article in a school magazine about going to an important tennis match. Answer the questions.

1 Who did Joanna go with?
2 Who did Joanna think would win?
3 Who won?
4 What did Joanna do after the match?

2 Find these words in the article. What does each word describe? Why does Joanna use them?

0	lucky	*my family*
1	full	_____
2	excited	_____
3	quite easy	_____
4	great	_____
5	fantastic	_____

3 ANALYSE Look at the three paragraphs of Joanna's article. Match the paragraphs with the contents.

Paragraph 1   a after the event
Paragraph 2   b introduction to the event
Paragraph 3   c details of the event (the match itself)

A QUESTION OF SPORT   UNIT 8

SPORTS NEWS

Home   About   Latest news

(1) Last Saturday was the final of the women's singles at the Wimbledon Championships, played (of course) at the All England Club (Wimbledon). My family were lucky enough to get tickets. When we got there, we went to the court and found our seats. Of course, the stadium was full and everyone was very excited. It was brilliant!

(2) At ten to two, the players came out: Venus Williams from the US and Garbiñe Muguruza from Spain. At first, I was sure Williams was going to win because she was a five-times Wimbledon champion, but as the match continued, it was clear that I was wrong. Both players played really well and after almost an hour, the exciting first set ended: 7-5 to Muguruza. Could 37-year-old Williams come back? No. She started to look tired and to play badly. The second set was quite easy for Muguruza, and after 20 minutes, she won the set 6–0 and won the match. At the age of 23, she was the new Wimbledon champion. The crowd stood and clapped and cheered. And then Muguruza got the trophy.

(3) After the match, we looked around a bit and then went home. We had a great time. The match was very exciting and it was fantastic to see a big sports event 'live'.

4 PLAN Think of a sports event that you went to or would like to go to. Answer the questions.

1 When is / was the event?
2 Where is / was it?
3 What is / was the atmosphere like (the crowd, the noise, etc.)?
4 What happens / happened at the event (players / goals / winners, etc.)?
5 How did / would you feel after the event (happy / tired / excited / unhappy)?

5 PRODUCE Write an article for a school magazine (about 120–150 words) about the sports event. Use Joanna's article and the language above to help you.

A2 Key for Schools

READING AND WRITING
Part 1: 3-option multiple choice

→ workbook page 71

1 For each question, choose the correct answer.

1
Men's bike for sale
Colour: red
2 years old
£300.00
Phone James
07867 534647

A The bike for sale is not for young children.
B The bike is not very good anymore.
C James is selling the bike because he doesn't like the colour.

2
Hi Karen
The Blue Tomatoes are playing in Hyde Park next Sunday. I'm going. The tickets are not cheap, but they're great! Come with me!
Sarah

A Sarah has got tickets for her and for Karen.
B Sarah hopes that Karen comes with her.
C Sarah hopes that Karen pays for her ticket.

3
Brighton Zoo
Half-price tickets this weekend: groups of 10 or more
Book online only

A You can get a discount on tickets by booking online or at the zoo.
B If you visit the zoo alone, tickets are more expensive.
C Only groups of ten or more can book zoo tickets this weekend.

4
Tony
Football practice starts at 5 pm. You have art class until 5:30. Shall we go together at 6? Meet me at the station.
Nick

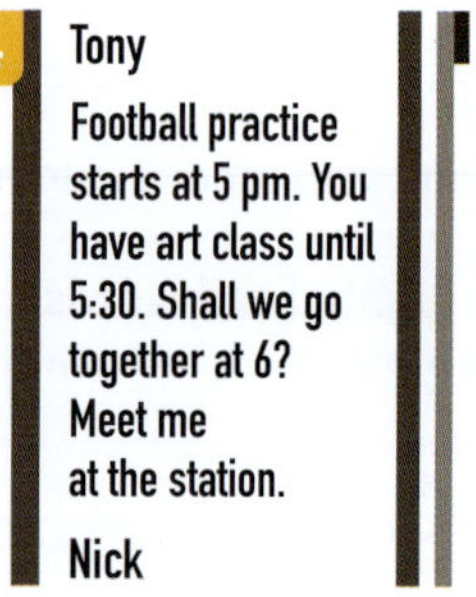

A Nick knows Tony can't be at football practice when it starts.
B Nick wants to go to football practice a bit earlier than Tony.
C Nick wants to be with Tony, but doesn't want to go to football practice.

5
Baking sale
Strawberry cakes
Buy one, get one free!
(Special offer 3–6 pm only!)

A The cake shop is only open after 3 pm.
B You can only get strawberry cakes from 3 to 6.
C Two cakes will cost the same as one.

6
Liz
Sorry you're ill. Don't forget the story writing competition. Miss Smith says we have to complete it by next Monday.
Love, Anne

Anne wrote this message
A to check if Liz finished her story.
B to let Liz know what they did in class today.
C to tell her about something she needs to do.

LISTENING
Part 4: 3-option multiple choice

→ workbook page 79

2 🔊 8.07 For each question, choose the correct answer.

1 You will hear a man talking to his son. What does the man want his son to do?
 A Finish his homework quickly.
 B Help him in the garden.
 C Work more carefully.

2 You will hear a girl, Kate, talking about shopping. Why did she buy the camera?
 A The colour was right.
 B The size was right.
 C The price was right.

3 You will hear a woman talking to her daughter. What's the weather like?
 A It's windy.
 B It's wet.
 C It's cold.

4 You will hear a teacher talking to her student, Sebastian. What is he going to do after school?
 A He's going to see the doctor.
 B He's going to help his parents.
 C He's going to visit his mother.

5 You will hear two friends talking about their day. What did they do?
 A They went to an adventure park.
 B They went cycling.
 C They went running.

TEST YOURSELF   UNITS 7 & 8

VOCABULARY

1 Complete the sentences with the words in the list. There are two extra words.

> basketball | calculator | does | hair dryer | headphones | make
> remote control | skiing | sailing | satnav | up | windsurfing

1 We're lost. We need a _____ .
2 I have to _____ my bed every morning before I go to school.
3 The kitchen's a mess. Someone should do the washing-_____ .
4 I love _____ . I've got a small boat and I go every weekend.
5 What is 319 divided by 11? That's hard. I need a _____ .
6 I was playing _____ when the ball hit me on the head.
7 I want to watch the news. Pass me the _____ , please.
8 My mum was _____ and she fell over in the snow three times!
9 Dad _____ the cooking in my house.
10 I'm trying to work and your music is too loud. Use your _____ , please.

/10

GRAMMAR

2 Complete the sentences with the past simple or past continuous form of the verbs.

> eat | find | see | stop | walk | watch

1 She _____ in the park when I saw her.
2 I was tidying my room when I _____ my favourite pen that I lost last week.
3 The docking station _____ working while we were listening to music.
4 We started running when we _____ the bus.
5 I _____ my dinner when the phone rang.
6 We _____ TV when Mum called us for dinner.

3 Find and correct the mistake in each sentence.

1 My mum and dad was playing in the garden with my brother.
2 You not have to go if you don't want to.
3 We mustn't run. The bus doesn't go for an hour.
4 You must to be careful. It's very dangerous.
5 She played football when she broke her leg.
6 Yesterday the sports shop was sell them for only £15.

/12

FUNCTIONAL LANGUAGE

4 Write the missing words.

1 A You _____ have to watch the film it if you don't want to.
  B Thanks, I don't _____ like it.
2 A I can't come out tonight. I've got lots of things to do.
  B Like _____ ?
  A Well, I've got to help my dad _____ the shopping, for a start.
3 A At _____ , I was a bit scared, but _____ a while I was OK.
4 A What _____ you doing at nine o'clock?
  B I was _____ the washing-up.

/8

MY SCORE /30

22–30 10–21 0–9

83

9 WILD AND WONDERFUL

OBJECTIVES

FUNCTIONS:
talking about the weather; paying compliments

GRAMMAR:
comparative adjectives; can / can't for ability; superlative adjectives

VOCABULARY:
geographical features; the weather; phrases with *with*

Get TH!NKING
Watch the video and think: what natural wonders do you see every day?

▶ 25

A
B 
C
D

READING

1 Look at the photos. Which of the animals can you name in English?

2 Name other animals in English. Write them down.

3 **SPEAKING** Work in pairs. Look at the animals on your list. What countries do you think of?

> *Lions come from South Africa.*

> *You find horses all over the world.*

4 **SPEAKING** Work in pairs. Look at the photos again and answer the questions.
  1 Do these animals live in hot or cold places?
  2 What do you think they eat?
  3 What dangers are there where they live?
  4 What is the relationship between these animals and people?
  5 Do people hunt these animals? Why or why not?
  6 What is interesting about these places for tourists?

5 🔊 9.01 Read and listen to the article. Mark the statements T (true) or F (false). Correct the false information.
  1 More than half the people in the world live in cities.
  2 When it rains in the Kalahari, the grass and the bushes turn from brown to green.
  3 The Chimbu skeleton dancers are the only tribe living near Mt Wilhelm.
  4 They paint skeletons on their bodies to scare away wild animals.
  5 The Nenets always go where the reindeer are.
  6 Young Kazakhs have to be strong to become golden eagle hunters.

6 **SPEAKING** Work in pairs or small groups. Think about and answer these questions.
  1 Would you like to go to the places in the article? Why (not)?
  2 Are you interested in the lives of people living in wild places? Why (not)?

> *I'd love to / I wouldn't like to … because …*

> *I'm (not) interested in …*

> *I think it's too dangerous to … / wonderful to …*

> *I love / hate reading about … watching documentaries about …*

WILD AND WONDERFUL UNIT 9

THE WILD
side of life

More and more people think that life is better in the city than the countryside. For the first time in history more than 50% of the world's population lives in urban areas. However, there are still many groups of people who live in some of the wildest places on the planet.

The Kalahari is a large area of bush land in southern Africa. It has two parts. The south part is drier than the north and plants do not grow there very well. Every year at the end of summer it rains and the land becomes more beautiful than at other times of the year. But the grass and the bushes soon get dry and turn brown again. Life there is difficult.

The San are a group of people who live in the Kalahari. They live in huts, eat wild animals – even lions – plants and berries. They are very good with bows and arrows, and use them for hunting.

Up in the mountains of central Papua New Guinea is the Chimbu Province. This jungle area is one of the world's most remote places. It is also home to Mt Wilhelm, the highest mountain on the island. Several different tribes live in the valleys between the mountains. One of these is the Chimbu skeleton dancers. They paint skeletons onto their bodies. This makes them look scarier and it frightens other people away from their land.

The Yamal Peninsula in northern Siberia is one and a half times bigger than France. It is frozen for much of the year and temperatures can reach -50°C in the winter. But this area is home to a tribe of about 10,000 people called the Nenets. The Nenets are nomadic, meaning they frequently move from one place to another. Each year around 300,000 reindeer move around the land and the Nenets always go with them. The recent discovery of gas in the area means more people than before are visiting the Yamal. So the Nenets now have more contact with the outside world.

The Bayan-Ölgii Province is the highest part of Mongolia. It is a wild area with many mountains, lakes, forests and rivers. It is also home to the Kazakh golden eagle hunters. These people travel around the mountains and use eagles to hunt for foxes and other small animals. When boys turn 13, they can become golden eagle hunters. However, they have to be stronger than most boys their age because they have to show that they can carry the weight of an eagle. There are about 100,000 Kazakh people, but only around 250 of them are golden eagle hunters.

TH!NK values

Valuing our world

7 Read and tick (✓) the statements that show that the natural world is important.

1 Why should I be interested in people living in wild places? There's nothing to learn from them. ☐

2 I want to organise trips to Papua New Guinea. People will pay a lot of money to see the skeleton dancers. ☐

3 It's great to learn about nature. It helps me to understand more about the world. ☐

4 Who needs wild animals? They're dangerous – and that's all! ☐

5 I watch a lot of nature programmes on TV. I support a project to save the tiger in India. ☐

8 SPEAKING Compare your ideas in pairs.

Statement 1 shows that the person does not know how wonderful our world is.

Why do you think that?

Because the person isn't interested in people living in wild places.

Maybe this person needs more information to understand how wonderful these places are.

GRAMMAR
Comparative adjectives

1 Look at the article on page 85. Find examples of comparisons. Then complete the table on the right.

	adjectives	comparative form
short adjectives (one syllable)	small hot big	⁰*smaller* (than) hotter (than) ¹_____ (than)
adjectives ending in consonant + -y	happy dry early	happier (than) ²_____ (than) earlier (than)
longer adjectives (two or more syllables)	attractive beautiful	more attractive (than) ³_____ (than)
irregular adjectives	bad good far	worse (than) ⁴_____ (than) farther / further (than)

2 Complete the sentences. Use the comparative form of the adjectives.

1 Africa is _____ (big) than Europe, but _____ (small) than Asia.
2 Be careful with the spiders in the Kalahari. They're _____ (dangerous) than in Europe.
3 Cars these days are _____ (good) quality than they were 30 years ago.
4 Sarah loves wildlife. For her, holidays in the Kalahari are _____ (interesting) than going to the seaside.
5 My sister has got two children. Her son is nine. His sister is two years _____ (young).
6 John is a musician. It's _____ (easy) for him to learn a new instrument than it is for me.

→ workbook page 82

VOCABULARY
Geographical features

3 🔊 9.02 Label the picture with the words. Write 1–12 in the boxes. Then listen and check.

1 beach | 2 desert | 3 forest | 4 hill | 5 island | 6 jungle | 7 lake | 8 mountain | 9 ocean | 10 river

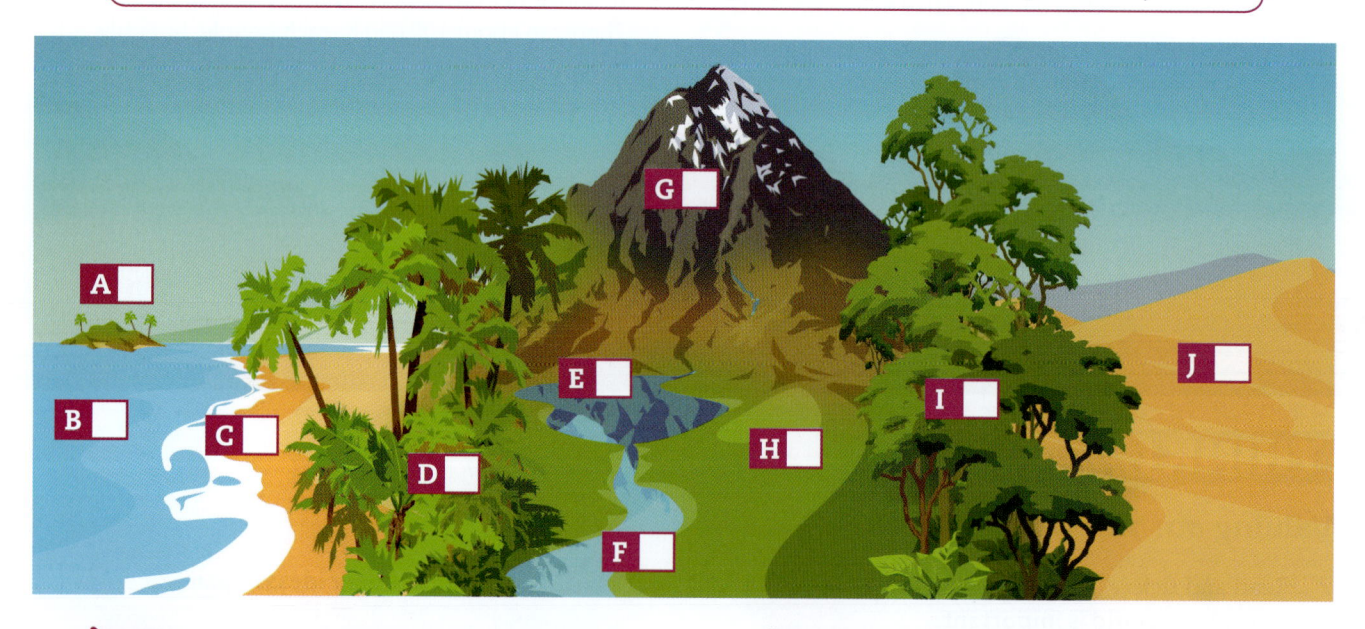

4 **SPEAKING** Work in pairs. Ask your partner to close their book and then ask them about the picture.

What's A?

I think it's … / I'm not sure if I can remember. Is it … ? / Can you give me the first letter, please?

5 **SPEAKING** Work in pairs. Compare some of the places. Use the adjectives in the list to help you, or use other adjectives.

beautiful | big | dangerous | difficult
exciting | high | hot | nice

A mountain is higher than a hill.

Yes, and it's more difficult to climb a mountain.

→ workbook page 84

WILD AND WONDERFUL   UNIT 9

LISTENING

6 Match the words in the list with the photos. Write 1–4 in the boxes.

1 vultures | 2 a lion and its kill
3 a spear | 4 antelopes

A
B
C
D

7 🔊 9.03 Listen to an interview with a Kalahari bushman. Which title best summarises the interview?

1 Life in the Kalahari
2 Lions, vultures and antelopes
3 A young man's difficult task
4 Big cats can't run fast

8 🔊 9.03 Listen again. For questions 1–5, tick (✓) A, B or C.

1 Where was PK born?
   A in the Kalahari
   B in the Sahara
   C in Kenya

2 Before a young man can get married, he has to
   A do a task.
   B find a lion.
   C kill an antelope.

3 It's important for the future family that the young man
   A kills many lions.
   B likes the girl's father.
   C has courage.

4 What can show the bushman where the lion is eating?
   A antelopes
   B vultures
   C his future family

5 To take the kill away from the lion, you have to
   A run faster than the lion can.
   B attack the lion with your spear.
   C be very quiet and surprise the lion.

Grammar rap!
▶26

GRAMMAR
can / can't for ability

9 Complete the sentences with *can* or *can't*.

1 How _____ you find a lion and its kill?
2 You _____ get the kill from the lion at night.
3 How _____ you get the meat away from the lion?

10 Complete the table.

Positive	I/you/we/they/he/she/it **can** run fast.
Negative	I/you/we/they/he/she/it ¹_____ (**cannot**) run fast.
Questions	²_____ I/you/we/they/he/she/it run fast?
Short answers	Yes, I/you/we/they/he/she/it **can**. No, I/you/we/they/he/she/it ³_____ (**cannot**).

11 Make sentences with *can* and *can't*.

0 Simon + run fast / – swim fast
   Simon can run fast, but he can't swim fast.
1 Matt + drive a car / – fly a plane
   Matt _____
2 I + write emails / – do Maths on my laptop
   I _____
3 They + write stories / – spell well
   They _____

→ workbook page 82

WordWise: Phrases with *with*

12 Match the parts of the sentences.

1 They are very good
2 The Nenets always go
3 The Nenets now have more contact
4 It's a wild area

a with the reindeer.
b with bows and arrows.
c with many mountains.
d with the outside world.

13 Put the words in the correct order.

1 friend / with / came / My / me / best
2 not / I'm / very / computers / with / good
3 with / very / I'm / homework / my / busy

→ workbook page 84

87

READING

1 🔊 9.04 Read and listen to the blog. Where was the biggest snowfall ever in one day? How much snow fell on that day?

EXTREME NATURE!

At 7.30 am on 22 January 1943, the people of Spearfish in South Dakota, US woke up to find the temperature outside was a freezing -20°C. Two minutes later, thermometers were showing a much warmer 7°C – a rise of 27°C in 120 seconds. But it didn't stop there. The temperature continued to go up and by 9 am it was 12°C. Just as the people started to think about enjoying a warm winter's day, the temperature fell 16°C in just under half an hour back down to -4°C and the residents had to put their coats back on! It was the most dramatic temperature change in the history of American weather.

The village of Capracotta is in the mountains near the Adriatic coast of Italy. It gets a lot of snow in the winter. But on 5 March 2015 its 1,000 inhabitants saw 256 cm of snowfall in 18 hours. It was the biggest snowfall ever in a day. One photo taken on the day shows a woman in a house shaking hands through the window with her neighbour in the street. The neighbour is standing on top of the snow. The woman is on the second floor of her home!

Do you like long sunny days? Then the best city in the world to live in is Reykjavik. 21 June is the longest day of the year in the northern hemisphere and the Icelandic capital gets 21 hours and 45 minutes of daylight. The sun hardly ever goes down. However, Reykjavik could also be the worst place to be. On the shortest day of the year, 21 December, the sun hardly rises there and people get only four hours and seven minutes of daylight. But during winter nights, you can often see the Northern Lights – one of the world's most beautiful natural events.

2 Read the blog again. Answer the questions.
1. How quickly did the temperature change from 12°C to -4°C in Spearfish?
2. What happened in Capracotta on 5 March 2015?
3. What makes the long winter nights in Reykjavik better?

SPEAKING

3 Work in pairs. Discuss these questions.
1. Which of the facts did you know before?
2. Which of the facts were new to you?
3. Which of the places mentioned would you like to visit most? Why?

4 Can you think of an amazing weather event in your country? Use the questions below to help you.

- Did a lot of snow fall?
- Did it rain heavily or was there a very strong wind?
- Was it very hot or was it very cold?
- Where were you that day? What did you do? How did you feel?

PRONUNCIATION
Vowel sounds: /ɪ/ and /aɪ/ Go to page 121. 🎧

WRITING
An email about an amazing weather event

5 Imagine you want to tell a friend about an amazing weather event. Write an email (100–125 words).
- Choose the place.
- In your email, say:
  – where the place is
  – what was special about the weather and when it happened
  – how the people reacted

GRAMMAR
Superlative adjectives

6 Put the words in order to make sentences. Check your answers in the article.
1. temperature change / the / of / was / the / American weather / It / in / most dramatic / history
2. day / snowfall / the biggest / was / ever / It / a / in
3. is / day of the year / 21 June / longest / the / in / hemisphere / the / northern
4. worst / be / Reykjavik / to / However / be / also / the / could / place

88

WILD AND WONDERFUL   UNIT 9

7 Look at the table. Complete the 'adjectives' column with the words in the list. Then complete the comparative and superlative forms.

bad | beautiful | happy | hot | ~~warm~~

	adjectives	comparative form	superlative form
short adjectives (one syllable)	0 _warm_ short long	warmer 5 _____ 6 _____	the warmest 14 _____ 15 _____
short adjectives ending in one vowel + one consonant	1 _____ big	hotter 7 _____	16 _____ 17 _____
adjectives ending in consonant + -y	sunny 2 _____	8 _____ happier	18 _____ 19 _____
longer adjectives (two or more syllables)	3 _____ difficult dramatic	more beautiful 9 _____ 10 _____	the most beautiful 20 _____ 21 _____
irregular adjectives	4 _____ good far	11 _____ 12 _____ 13 _____	the worst 22 _____ 23 _____

8 Complete the sentences. Use the superlative form of the adjectives.

0 It's Cindy's birthday tomorrow. She's ____the happiest____ (happy) girl in class.
1 Brazil is _____ (big) country in South America.
2 I had an awful headache this morning. I think I did _____ (bad) test ever.
3 I think social media is _____ (good) way of contacting people.
4 She's great at Maths. She can solve _____ (difficult) sums.

→ workbook page 83

VOCABULARY
The weather

9 🔊 9.07 Write the words under the pictures. Listen and check.

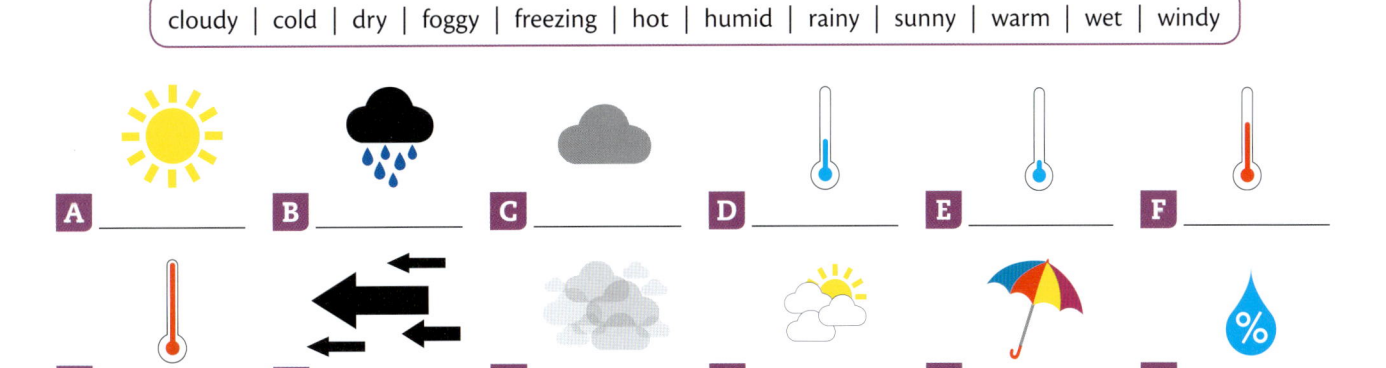

cloudy | cold | dry | foggy | freezing | hot | humid | rainy | sunny | warm | wet | windy

A _____ B _____ C _____ D _____ E _____ F _____

G _____ H _____ I _____ J _____ K _____ L _____

10 Think about the different kinds of weather. Write reasons why you think they can be good.

a sunny day: We can ride our bikes.
a hot day: We can go swimming.
a rainy day: We can play computer games.

11 SPEAKING Work in pairs. Make dialogues about the weather with a partner.

What a nice day.
Yes, it's really warm. Let's ride our bikes.
Great idea.

→ workbook page 84

89

DEVELOPING SPEAKING

1 🔊 9.08 Look at the photo. What do you think is happening? Why? Listen and read to check.

James:	Excuse me. Can we get our ball, please?
Alice:	Yes, of course.
James:	Oh, what a lovely garden!
Alice:	Thank you. That's a nice thing to say. Do you like gardening, then?
James:	Well, not really. I don't know much about flowers and things. But my sister loves them, don't you, Gill?
Gill:	That's right. And your flowers really look wonderful. I love your roses.
Alice:	Thank you again. I do it all myself, you know. My husband helped me before, but he can't walk very well now, so I have to do it all. It's a lot of work. I get very, very tired.
Gill:	Well, we can help you – can't we, James?
James:	We're in the middle of a game and I'm winning! Maybe another day.
Gill:	We can finish our game later, James. What would you like us to do?
Alice:	What nice people you are! Well, perhaps you can help me move the table and chairs under that tree. They're in the sun at the moment and it's very hot. But first, I just need to make a phone call and a cup of tea. I'll be back in a minute.
James:	No problem. We're fine here. OK. Let's move the table first. We can do that together. Then the chairs.
moments later …	
Alice:	Oh, that's fantastic. Well done! Look, let me give you some money for some ice cream or chocolate. To say thank you.
Gill:	No, please. We're happy to help. Come on, James. Bye!
James:	How nice! She wanted to give us some money!
Gill:	I know. And I feel so good now. I don't want ice cream, or chocolate, either. Her smile was enough.
James:	That's right. But let's get some ice cream anyway!

2 🔊 9.08 Read and listen again and answer the questions.

1 What does James say about Alice's garden?
2 Why does Alice's husband not help her?
3 What does Alice ask them to do?
4 Why does Alice want to give them money?
5 Why does Gill say 'no' to Alice's money?

3 Imagine you were in James and Gill's situation. Would you take the money that Alice wants to give them? Why (not)?

Phrases for fluency

4 Find the expressions 1–5 in the dialogue. Who says them? How do you say them in your language?

0 … in a minute.   *Alice*
1 Well done!   _____
2 … , either.   _____
3 No problem.   _____
4 … , not really.   _____
5 … , then?   _____

5 Complete the conversations with the expressions in Exercise 4.

1 **A** I got 97% in the test, Dad.
   B _____ ! Did you study hard for it, _____ ?
2 **A** Hi, David. I can't talk right now. Sorry. I'll phone you _____ , OK?
   B _____ , Chris. Call me back when you can.
3 **A** Did you enjoy the film?
   B No, _____ . I didn't like the book very much, _____ .

FUNCTIONS
Paying compliments

KEY LANGUAGE
What a lovely … !   … really looks wonderful.   I love …

6 Use the words from the Key Language box to write compliments.

1 Your friend is wearing a new jacket that you think is lovely.
   You: _____ !
2 Your friend is drawing a very nice picture. You really like it.
   You: _____ .
3 Your friend has got a new hairstyle and you really like it.
   You: _____ !

7 Work in pairs. Use the photos to make compliments.

What a lovely voice!

WILD AND WONDERFUL   UNIT 9

LIFE COMPETENCIES

We all belong to communities – our family, our school, our town, our country – and there is always something everybody thinks should be better for that community. It's easy to do nothing and wait for other people to help. Helping our community isn't always easy, but it feels good.

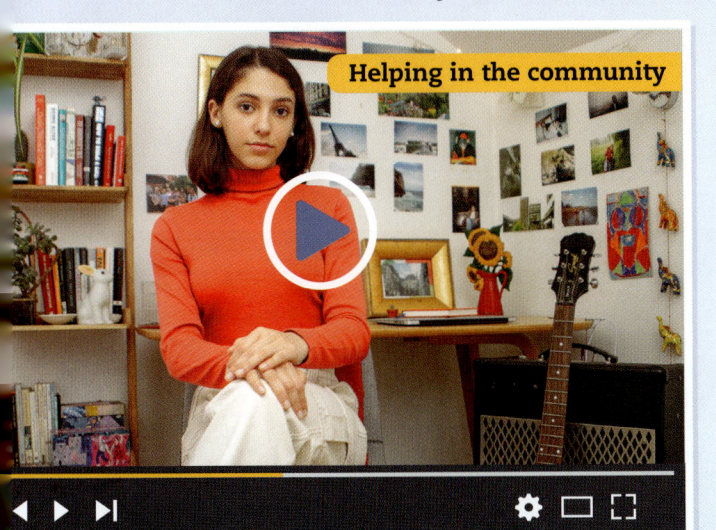

Helping in the community

1 ▶ 27 Watch the video. How many neighbours does she talk about? How does she help her community?

2 ▶ 27 Watch again and answer the questions.

1 Who gives her the project?
2 How does she feel when he gets the project?
3 What is the project?
4 What does she learn about:
  a Mr Rodgers?
  b Mrs Thomas?
  c Mr Saunders?
5 How does she feel about the project now?

3 Read about the Under the Tree Foundation. What does it do?

4 Work in pairs. Choose a community. Write all the difficulties you can think of for people in that community. Use the examples to help you.

Your country – homeless people …
The world – places with no clean water …
Your town/local area – rubbish on the streets …
Your school – books in your classroom need organising …
Your family – the car is dirty …

5 Exchange and share your ideas with another pair who wrote about a different community. Then write ideas on ways your class can help with these problems.

Me and my world

6 SPEAKING Tick (✓) the sentences that are true for you. Compare with a partner.

☐ I know most of the people where I live.
☐ I talk to my neighbours almost every day.
☐ There is a good community spirit where I live.
☐ I sometimes help with local projects.
☐ I'd like to be more involved in my local community.
☐ A happy community is good for everyone.

TIPS FOR HELPING IN THE COMMUNITY

- Identify what you are not happy about in your community and think of ways of improving it.
- Always put the objectives of the community above your personal goals.
- Don't be afraid to offer your own suggestions, but listen and consider the opinions of others.

When he was 12, Jonathan Woods went Christmas shopping and had a great idea. He was buying toys to give to an organisation in his town. They gave the toys to young children whose parents didn't have enough money to buy Christmas presents. While he was looking for presents to buy, he had a thought. The organisation helped young children, but many older children his age were probably in the same situation as the young children. Who was buying presents for them?

Jonathan decided to start an organisation to buy Christmas presents for older children. He called it the Under the Tree Foundation. He also asked an organisation working with older children and teenagers in his local area for advice on what to buy.

In 2007, Jonathan sent letters to all his friends and family asking them to help Under the Tree. The response to these letters was fantastic. Twenty-five older children received the presents they'd wanted for Christmas, and over 80 teenagers were invited to a pizza and movie night.

The next year, Under the Tree bought presents for over 50 children. The organisation still continues to help older children have a better Christmas.

91

10 OUT AND ABOUT

OBJECTIVES

FUNCTIONS:
talking about plans; inviting and making arrangements; discussing ideas for an imaginary film

GRAMMAR:
be going to for intentions; present continuous for arrangements; adverbs

VOCABULARY:
places in a town; things in town: compound nouns

Get TH!NKING

Watch the video and think: what is unique about your town?

A

B

C

D

READING

1 Look at the photos. In which one can you see these things? Where are the places?
1 a very famous **statue**
2 a **sports stadium**
3 a really long **wall**
4 a **park** in a city centre

2 SPEAKING Work in pairs. Name more places you can find in a town.

museum, shop, station

3 SPEAKING How important are these places for a town? Think about who each place is important for and why. Compare your ideas with another pair.

4 Work in pairs. Discuss the questions.
1 What interesting places for tourists are there in your town or city?
2 What interesting events for tourists are there?

5 🔊 10.01 Read and listen to the emails. Answer the questions.
1 Where are the writers writing from?
2 What do they think of the places?
3 What is different about the two people writing these emails?

6 🔊 10.01 Read and listen to the emails again and mark the sentences A (true), B (false) or C (doesn't say).
1 Ryan had problems with his flight.
   A True B False C Doesn't say
2 Ryan is in a band and they are going to play in a famous concert hall.
   A True B False C Doesn't say
3 Ryan's band is the only one from Europe.
   A True B False C Doesn't say
4 Bettina and her team lost the match against the under-15 Beijing champions.
   A True B False C Doesn't say
5 Bettina would like to see the Great Wall, but she can't because she has to go back to Beijing.
   A True B False C Doesn't say
6 She cannot play volleyball for six weeks.
   A True B False C Doesn't say

OUT AND ABOUT UNIT 10

Mum
Mrs_hudson@thinkmail.com

Hi Mum!!

Hi Mum,

It's Day Two and I'm already in love with New York. It's amazing. The first day, we were pretty tired from the flight, but we did a bit of sightseeing in the afternoon. We went to see the Statue of Liberty and I wasn't disappointed. We had a guided tour and learned all about its history. It really is a powerful symbol of peace.

Today, we're going to explore Central Park and Manhattan. In the evening, we're going to watch the New York Jets. They're playing at MetLife Stadium. It's my first game of American football and I'm looking forward to it. (I think – I'm quite nervous!)

The big concert we're playing in is tomorrow and we're all getting quite excited. Just imagine, I'm going to play my trombone in Carnegie Hall, probably the most famous concert hall in the US. Mr Davis is even more excited. He's going to conduct us in the concert. He keeps telling us it's his dream come true. His wife's going to record the performance. She's going to send us all the link so you can see the greatest moment of my musical career so far! There are going to be bands from all over the world, from about 20 different countries. I can't wait!

Hope you're well and not missing me too much!

Love,

Ryan

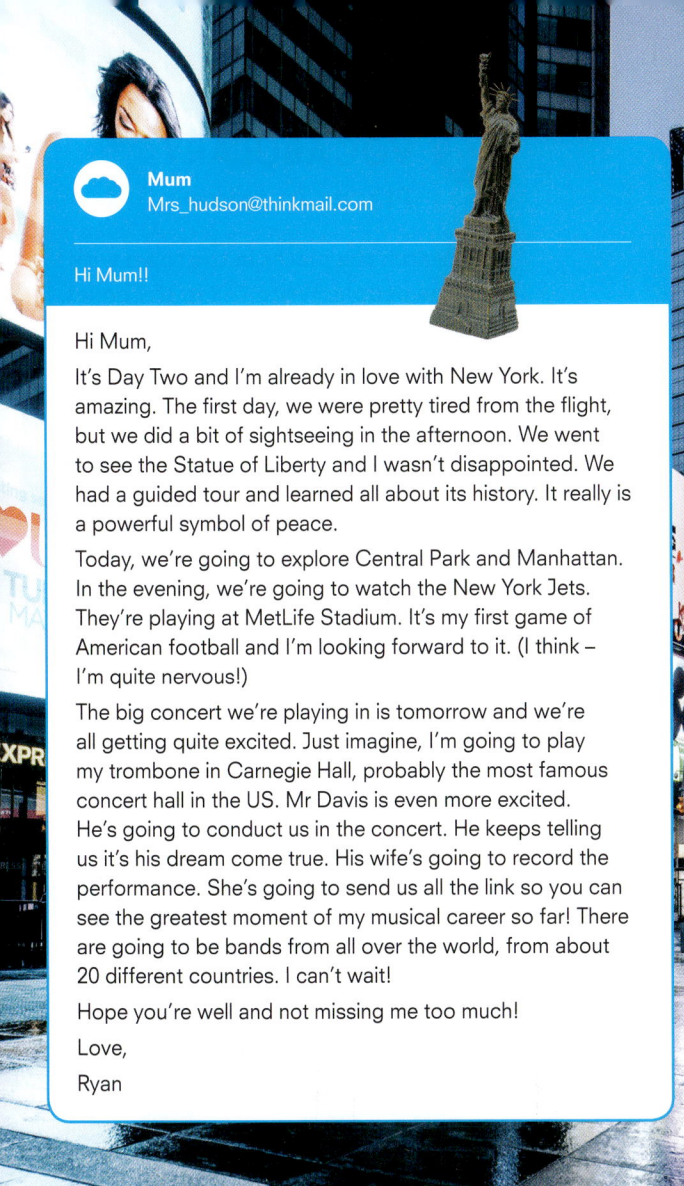

Abigail
abi@mymail.com

China!

Hi Abigail,

Sorry I didn't write yesterday, but it was such a busy day I just didn't get the time. We played our second volleyball match of the trip. It was against the under-15 Beijing champions and they won easily. I also hurt my hand quite badly. The sports centre where we played was fantastic. Really modern and much better than ours back home. Anyway, I've got ten minutes to write to you quickly, then I'm going to the bus station to catch a bus to Luanping. I'm so excited because we're going to visit the Great Wall. It was probably the one thing I wanted to do most on this trip, after playing volleyball, of course! 😊 We're going to explore the Jinshanling section of the wall. It's in the mountains and it's quite a walk to get up to it. But the views are spectacular. I'm going to take loads of photos. Luanping is about 130 km away, so we're going to spend the night there. Then we're going back to Beijing for our last day in the city. Our last match is in the afternoon, but I'm not going to play because of my hand. I can't believe the trip is almost over. China is amazing and the Chinese people are so friendly. I want to stay longer.

Lots of love,

Bettina

TH!NK values

Appreciating other cultures

7 Read and tick (✓) the things you do.

You are on an exchange trip in a new country for two weeks. Which of these things would you do?

- ☐ Make friends with the local children.
- ☐ Try and find children from your own country who are also on holiday there.
- ☐ Try and learn some of the local language.
- ☐ Speak your own language (and hope people understand you).
- ☐ See if the TV has programmes from your own country.
- ☐ Read the books you brought from home.
- ☐ Visit the museums.
- ☐ Listen to and buy some music by musicians from that country.

8 SPEAKING Work in pairs. Decide which of the things in Exercise 7 are good to help you find out more about a different culture. What other things can you think of that are also good to do?

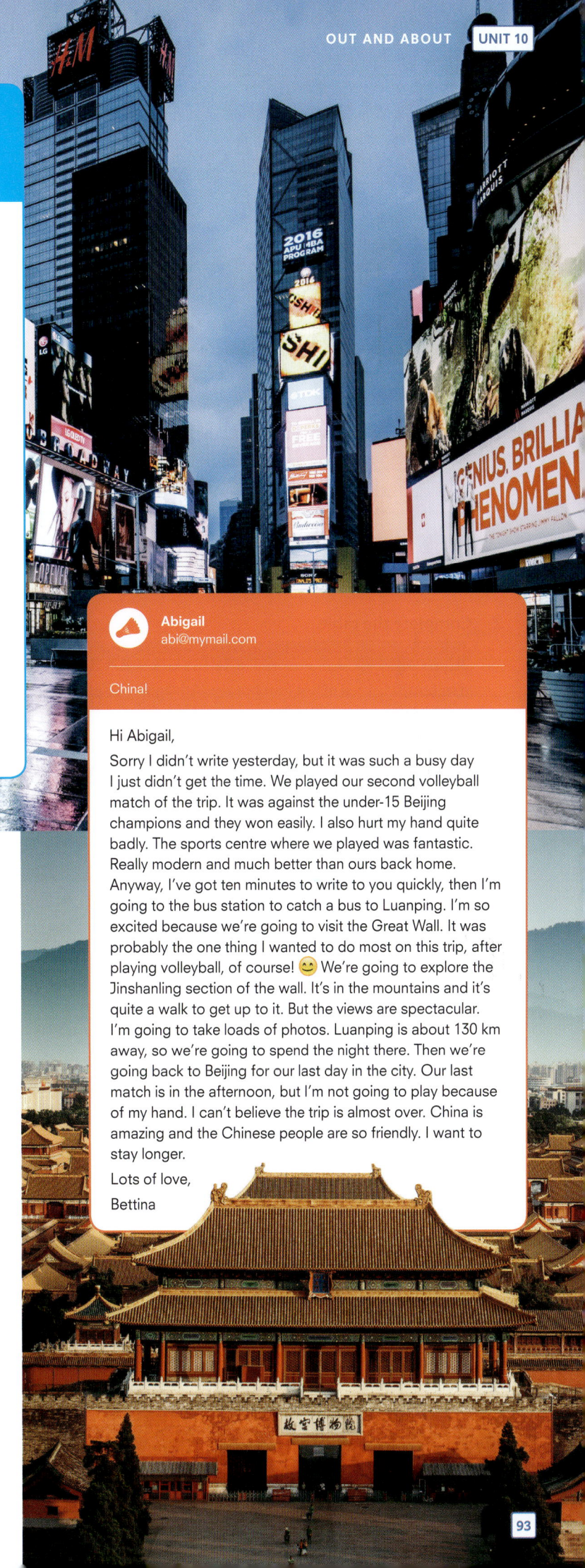

Grammar rap! ▶29

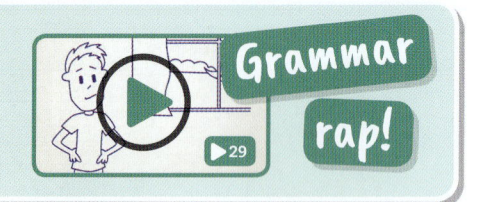

GRAMMAR
be going to for intentions

1 **Complete the sentences from the emails on page 93 with the correct form of *be*. Then complete the rule.**

0 I '**m**___ going to take loads of photos.
1 Today, we _____ going to explore Central Park.
2 His wife _____ going to record the performance.
3 There _____ going to be bands from all over the world.
4 We _____ going to visit the Great Wall.

> **RULE:** We use **be going to** to talk about our intentions for the [5]*future* / *present*. Use the present tense of *be* + *going to* + [6]*base form* / *-ing form* of the verb.

2 **Complete the table.**

Positive	Negative	Questions	Short answers
I'm (am) going to play.	I'm not (am not) going to play.	Am I going to play?	Yes, [5]_____. No, I'm not.
You/we/they're (are) going to play.	You/we/they [1]_____ (are not) going to play.	[3]_____ you/we/they going to play?	Yes, you/we/they [6]_____. No, you/we/they aren't.
He/she/it's (is) going to play.	He/she/it [2]_____ (is not) going to play.	[4]_____ he/she/it going to play?	Yes, he/she/it is. No, he/she/it [7]_____.

3 **Complete the future intentions with the correct form of the verbs.**

> ~~not watch~~ | take | not fight | not borrow | eat

0 I _I'm not going to watch_ so much TV.
1 My parents _____ out more often.
2 My brother _____ with me anymore.
3 I _____ the dog for a walk every day.
4 My sisters _____ my clothes without asking anymore.

4 **Look at the table. Tick (✓) the things you are going to do.**

tonight	this week	this year
do homework	play sport	write a blog
watch TV	visit relatives	have a holiday
tidy your room	play a computer game	learn something new

5 **SPEAKING** Ask and answer questions about the activities above.

> Are you going to watch TV tonight?
> Yes, I am.

→ workbook page 90

VOCABULARY
Places in town

6 **Match the places in the town with the people. Write 1–8 in the boxes.**

> 1 concert hall | 2 sports centre
> 3 shopping mall | 4 bus station
> 5 police station | 6 post office
> 7 football stadium | 8 car park

7 **SPEAKING** Work in pairs. Describe a place from Exercise 6 for your partner to guess.

> You go here to buy clothes.

→ workbook page 92

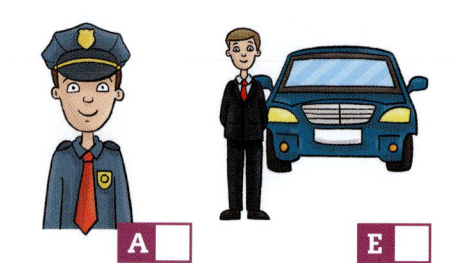

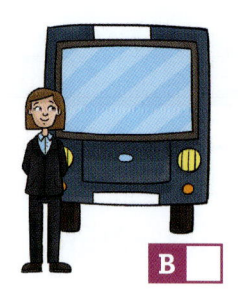

A
B
C
D
E
F
G
H

94

LISTENING

8 🔊 10.02 Listen to Olivia and Connor. When is the History test?

9 🔊 10.02 Listen again and mark the statements T (true) or F (false).
1 Connor has an important football match on Saturday.
2 Connor is celebrating his birthday at an American restaurant.
3 Olivia is not a fan of superhero films.
4 Connor invites Olivia to the museum.
5 Connor has about an hour between getting back from the museum and his piano lesson.
6 Connor isn't very busy the following weekend.

GRAMMAR
Present continuous for arrangements

10 Look at the examples. Choose the correct options.
1 What *are you doing / do you do* this weekend?
2 Dad's *taking / takes* me to the sports centre. We're *going to watch / watch* the basketball game.

11 Complete the rule with the words in the list.

present | future | arrangements

RULE: We can use the ¹_____ continuous to talk about ²_____ for the ³_____ .

12 Complete the sentences. Use the present continuous form of the verb.
0 I __'m going__ (go) to Dan's party on Saturday.
1 Oliver _____ (not come) to my house this afternoon.
2 Jessica and I _____ (do) our homework together after school.
3 We _____ (not visit) my grandparents on Sunday.
4 _____ your class _____ (go) on a trip next week?
5 My brother _____ (play) in the basketball final on Monday.

13 Complete the conversation. Use the present continuous form of the verbs in the list.

not do (x2) | go | buy | meet | do (x2) | play

Kenny What ¹_____ you _____ this afternoon?
Elena Nothing. I ²_____ anything.
Kenny Paul and I ³_____ football. Do you want to come?
Elena OK. Can I invite Tim? He ⁴_____ anything, either.
Kenny Sure. And what about your brother? ⁵_____ he _____ anything?
Elena Yes, he ⁶_____ shopping with my mum. They ⁷_____ his birthday present.
Kenny OK. Well, we ⁸_____ Jack, Adam, Lucy and Julia at the park at two.
Elena OK. See you at two, then.

→ workbook page 90

FUNCTIONS
Inviting and making arrangements

14 Put the words in order to make sentences. Which sentences are accepting an invitation? Which ones are refusing?
1 like / with / you / Would / to / come / us
2 love / to / I'd
3 study / Do / want / together / to / you
4 sorry / I'm / can't / I
5 great / That / be / would

15 Complete the exchanges.
1 A Would _____ go to the cinema with me?
   B _____ great.
2 A I'm going to the shops. Do _____ come with me?
   B I'm sorry. I _____ . I've got a lot to do.
3 A _____ like _____ meet up on Sunday?
   B Sunday? Yes. I _____ to.

16 Think of three arrangements and write them in your diary.

Saturday — Morning / Afternoon
Sunday — Morning / Afternoon

17 Can you complete your diary? Walk around the classroom and:
1 invite people to do things with you.
2 find things to do when you're free.

| A | |  B | |  C |

| Home | About | **Latest posts** |

As you probably know, the town council have got £1 million to spend on improving the town's facilities for young people and we're looking for great ideas on how to spend the money well. Post your ideas in the forum below and let us know how we can make life better for you.

1 There's nothing for teenagers to do in this town, especially at night. Can we use the money to build a youth club? Somewhere with a pool table and a table tennis table, perhaps. We need somewhere to play happily and hang out safely in the evenings. *Daisy, 15*

2 As I'm only 14, I can't drive, so I go everywhere on my bike. But the roads are dangerous and many motorists drive too fast. How about spending the money on building more cycle lanes? We could also put in more speed cameras and zebra crossings, too. This will make life safer for all our citizens, not just the young people. *Liz, 14*

3 I think the best use for the money is to build a playground in the town park. It should have lots of rides for the young kids but also stuff for teenagers, too. I'd like to see a graffiti wall and a skateboard park for a start and maybe if there is enough money, we can have a climbing wall, too. *Luke, 13*

4 Our high street is full of empty shops because everyone just shops at the new shopping centre outside of town or online. Why don't we use the money to turn some of these empty shops into an arts centre? It can have studios where we can draw and paint or learn how to make films. We could also have a music studio where local bands can record music cheaply. *Alex, 17*

5 How about a big billboard at the entrance to the town that reads, 'TEEN WARNING – there's nothing to do here!' *Sadie, 16*

6 This probably sounds like a boring idea, but can't we use some of the money to buy more litter bins? I feel ashamed of our town when I see all the litter on the ground. We need to tidy up our town quickly! *Jack, 15*

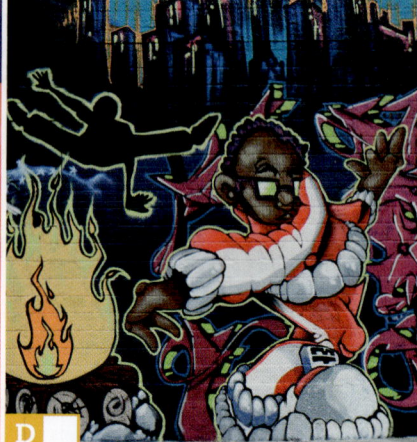

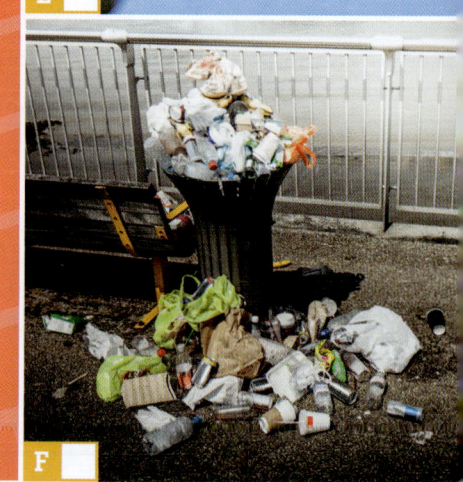

| D | | E | | F |

READING

1 Look at the photos. Which of them show problems? What are the problems?

2 🔊 10.03 Read and listen to the forum. Match the texts with the photos.

3 Read the entries again. Answer the questions.
1. Why are these young people writing on the forum?
2. What does Daisy think young people need in the town?
3. What does Liz think is missing?
4. Why are there so many empty buildings on the high street?
5. What does Jack think is a big problem in the town?

OUT AND ABOUT | UNIT 10

Train to TH!NK

Problem solving

4 SPEAKING Work in pairs. Read and discuss the problem.

The young people in your town aren't happy. They say there is nothing to do.
Make a list of suggestions to help solve this problem.

have a music festival   build a skateboard park

5 Think about your suggestions. What are the advantages and disadvantages of each one?

Suggestions	😊	😔
music festival	young people love music / fun	noisy / make a mess / expensive

6 SPEAKING Decide which suggestion you think is the best. Compare your ideas with the rest of the class.

> We think a musical festival is the best idea because all young people love music. It's also a lot of fun.

GRAMMAR
Adverbs

7 Look at the sentences from the website on page 96. Make a list of adjectives and adverbs.

0 We're looking for great ideas on how to spend the money well. *Adjective: great Adverb: well*
1 We need somewhere to play happily and hang out safely in the evenings.
2 Many motorists drive too fast.
3 Our high street is full of empty shops.
4 We could also have a music studio where local bands can record music cheaply.
5 This probably sounds like a boring idea.
6 We need to tidy up our town quickly!

8 Complete the rule.

> **RULE:** To form adverbs:
> - add [1]_____ to regular adjectives (e.g., *quick* ➔ *quickly*).
> - delete the *-y* and add [2]_____ to adjectives ending in consonant + *-y*. (e.g., *happy* ➔ *happily*).
> Some adjectives have irregular adverb forms.
> e.g., *fast* ➔ *fast*   *good* ➔ [3]_____
> Adverbs usually come immediately after the object of the verb or the verb (if there is no object).
> *He plays tennis **well**.* NOT ~~He plays well tennis.~~

9 Complete the sentences. Choose the correct words and write them in the correct form.

0 His car was really _fast_. He won the race _easily_. (easy / fast)
1 It's not _____. You need to do it very _____. (careful / easy)
2 We need to walk _____. I don't want to be _____. (late / quick)
3 I did my homework _____. I was really _____. (tired / bad)
4 He drives really _____. I get quite _____ in the car with him. (scared / dangerous)

➔ workbook page 91

VOCABULARY
Things in town: compound nouns

10 Choose a word from A and a word from B to make things you can find in a town. Look at the website on page 96 to help you.

> **A** bill | cycle | graffiti | high litter | ~~speed~~ | youth | zebra
> **B** bin | board | ~~camera~~ | club crossing | lane | street | wall

11 Complete the sentences with the words in Exercise 10.

0 Slow down. There's a _speed camera_ just ahead.
1 I really like that _____ advertising the new Italian restaurant has in town.
2 Don't drop your paper on the ground. There's a _____ behind you.
3 Don't try and cross the road here – there's a _____ just down there.
4 We live in a flat above one of the shops in the _____ .
5 The new _____ is really popular. Loads of people are painting on it.
6 I ride my bike to school. There's a _____ from outside my house all the way there.
7 We go to the _____ every Friday night. I usually play table tennis and chat with my friends there.

➔ workbook page 92

PRONUNCIATION
Voiced /ð/ and unvoiced /θ/ consonants
Go to page 121.

97

Culture

TH!NK — Mythical places around the world

1. Look at the pictures. What do you think a mythical place is?

2. Read the article quickly. Where are each of the places?

3. 🔊 10.06 Read the article again and listen. Mark the sentences T (true) or F (false).
   1. Many people have heard about Atlantis, but it is not very clear where and what it is.
   2. The legend says that the people of Atlantis were famous for their culture and education.
   3. Jules Verne knew where to find Agartha.
   4. People believed that El Dorado was made of gold.
   5. Plato was the first person to write about the island of Thule.
   6. There is a story that Thule is a dark place, but a lot of great food grows there.

Mythical PLACES AROUND THE WORLD

There are very few places on Earth that are undiscovered and we have satellite photos of the most remote places on the planet. But people are always interested in mythical lands, places that people say exist but no one has ever found.

Perhaps the most famous mythical place of all is **Atlantis**. Some people say it is a city, others say it is an island and others call it a continent. But whatever it is exactly, there is one thing that everyone agrees on: it is underneath the sea. The Greek philosopher Plato was the first person to describe it and he suggested that one time, its people attacked Athens. No one is sure exactly where Atlantis is. Because of its name, some people think it is somewhere in the Atlantic Ocean. Others say it's in the Mediterranean Sea or in the Caribbean.

Agartha is another mythical place that is not on the land. The legend says that it's at the centre of our planet. Like Atlantis, it is famous for its culture and educated society. It was the inspiration for Jules Verne's novel *Journey to the Centre of the Earth*. It tells the story of a group of travellers who go on an exciting adventure underground. Many people have tried to find the entrance to Agartha, which they think is somewhere in Antarctica.

Some people believe that somewhere in South America there is a famous city of gold: **El Dorado**. Many people tried to find it, but they weren't successful. El Dorado was originally the name of a person, a ruler of the ancient Colombian society called the Muisca. He covered himself in gold powder every day. There were legends in which people imagined that the whole city was made of gold.

Our final mythical land is an island called **Thule**. The legend says that it is in the north of the Earth, somewhere between Norway and Iceland. This is an area of the world that is completely dark for a lot of the year. But the story goes that Thule is a place where a lot of delicious food grows and people are always happy. The Roman poet Silius Italicus wrote about Thule. In his story, the people living there are painted blue.

OUT AND ABOUT UNIT 10

4 **VOCABULARY** There are six highlighted words in the article. Match the words with these meanings. Write the words.

0 not real, with lots of stories about it — *mythical*
1 a large group of people who live together in an organised way _____
2 leader of a country or kingdom _____
3 far away from people and places _____
4 without light _____
5 an old story _____

5 **SPEAKING** Work in pairs. Discuss.

1 Imagine you are going to make a film set in one of these mythical places. Think about the following:
   - What kind of film is it? (horror, love, science fiction?)
   - What's the story about briefly? (It's about a …)
   - Who is going to star in your film? (It's going to star my favourite actors …)
2 Present your ideas to the group and vote on the best idea.

WRITING
An informal email

1 **INPUT** Read the email. Answer the questions.
   1 Where is Emily going to spend her summer holidays?
   2 What is she going to do there?

2 Find these expressions in the email. Use them to answer the questions below.

> Guess what? | You won't believe it.
> I can't wait. | By the way, … | Anyway, …

   1 Which two expressions do we use to change topic?
   2 Which two expressions do we use to introduce some surprising news?
   3 Which expression means 'I'm really excited'?

3 **ANALYSE** Look at paragraphs 1 and 2 of Emily's email. Match the functions with the paragraphs. Write a–d.

   Paragraph 1: _____ and _____
   Paragraph 2: _____ and _____

   a Describe the city
   b Give news
   c Ask how your friend is
   d Talk about your plans

4 What is the function of paragraph 3?

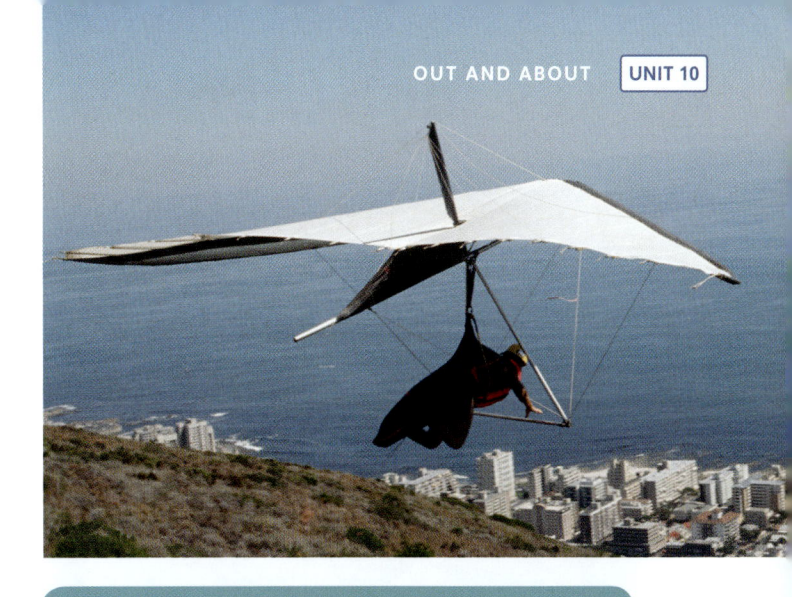

Luke
luckyluke@writeme.co.uk

Exciting news!

Hi Luke,

[1] How are you? I hope you're not studying too hard. Don't worry, there are only two more weeks of school. Anyway, I'm writing because I've got some really cool news. You won't believe it. Mum and Dad are taking me to Cape Town for the summer. Cape Town, South Africa! I can't wait.

[2] So I did some research on the internet. It looks like a really amazing place. Of course, there's the famous Table Mountain and the waterfront markets, but there are so many other great things to do there. I'm definitely going to go on a safari. And guess what? Mum's going to buy me some hang-gliding lessons. I'm going to be a hang-glider! We're going to be there for the whole of August. It's winter there, but I think the South African winter is hotter than our summer. So that's it – my big news. What do you think?

[3] By the way, Dad says we're going to be in Newquay next weekend. Is there any chance we can meet up? Let me know.

Love,
Emily

5 Which paragraph answers these questions?
   a What famous mountain is there in Cape Town?
   b What's your news?
   c How long are you going to stay in Cape Town?
   d What's the weather like in Cape Town?
   e What are you going to do in Cape Town?
   f Where are you going?

6 **PRODUCE** Imagine you are going to spend your next holiday in a famous city. Write an email (about 100–120 words) to your friend telling her the news.
   - Use the questions in Exercise 5 to help you.
   - Use some of the language in Exercise 2.

A2 Key for Schools

READING AND WRITING
Part 7: Picture story → workbook page 61

1. Look at the three pictures. Write the story shown in the pictures. Write 35 words or more.

Part 5: Open cloze

2. For each question, write the correct answer. Write **one** word for each gap.
→ workbook page 43

My name ⁰ _is_ Hugo. I live in the north of Wales in a town called Llandudno. My town has ¹_____ unusual name because it's Welsh. I ²_____ born here, so I speak Welsh really well. I think Llandudno is ³_____ most beautiful town in Wales. It's by the sea and I love ⁴_____ go swimming.
In Llandudno, there ⁵_____ parks, a small mountain with a café at the top, and a really good concert hall where great bands play. Every Friday night I meet ⁶_____ my friends to play games and have some fun in Llandudno.

LISTENING
Part 2: Gap fill → workbook page 79

3. 🔊 10.07 For each question, write the correct answer in the gap. Write one word or a number or a date or a time.

You will hear some information about a shopping centre. Listen and complete each question.

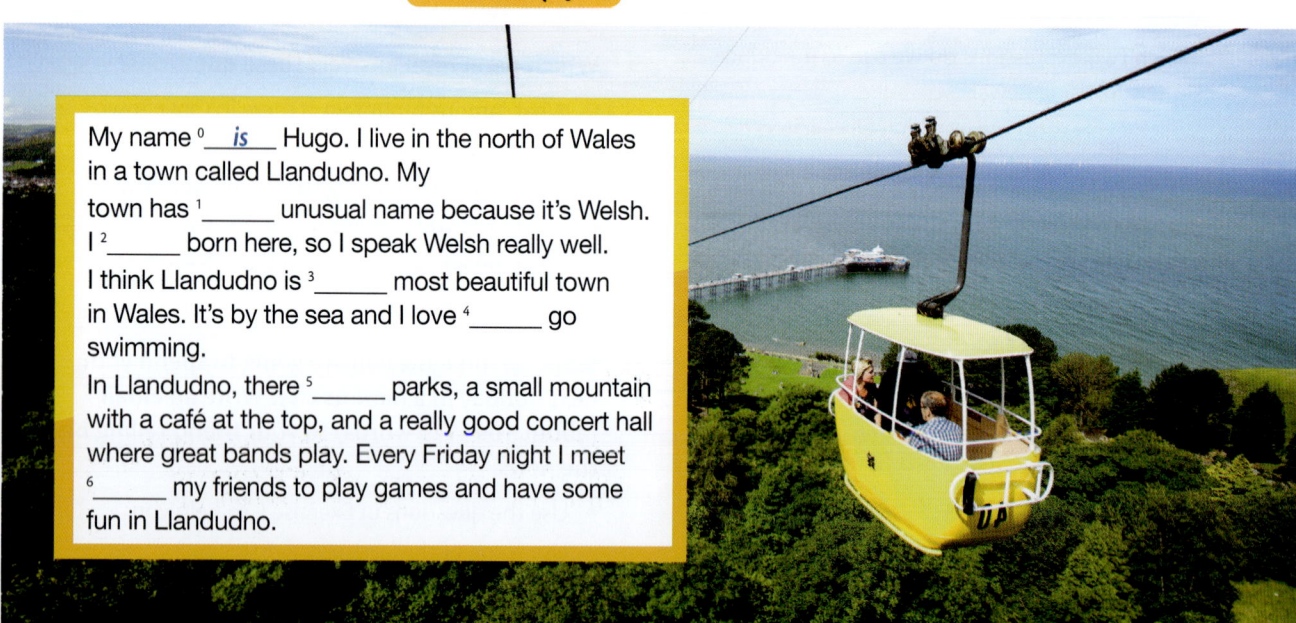

Blue Water Shopping Centre

- **Number of shops:** ⁰ _300_
- Restaurants and a ¹_____ on fifth floor
- **Parking:** £²_____ per hour
- Buses to the city centre every ³_____ minutes
- Shops open until 7.30 – every day except ⁴_____
- **Website:** ⁵_____

TEST YOURSELF

UNITS 9 & 10

VOCABULARY

1 Complete the sentences with the words in the list. There are two extra words.

bin | cloudy | hall | house | island | lake | lanes | mountains | station | sunny | windy | zebra

1 It's very _____ today. You can't see the sun at all.
2 We live on a small _____ . We're always close to the sea.
3 Mum and Dad are going to the concert _____ tonight. They love classical music.
4 It's one of the highest _____ in the world and it took the climbers three days to get to the top.
5 It's so _____ that my hat just blew off my head.
6 Don't try and cross the road here. There's a _____ crossing just up there.
7 It's easy to get about town on a bike because there are cycle _____ everywhere.
8 Someone stole my bike last night. I went to the police _____ , but they say it's hard to find stolen bikes.
9 Put your rubbish in the litter _____ over there.
10 We went swimming in the _____ – the water was really cold!

/10

GRAMMAR

2 Put the words in order to make sentences.

1 going / She's / nine / to / me / at / phone
2 Friday / We're / afternoon / on / leaving
3 homework / carefully / her / did / very / She
4 bag / I / remember / my / where / can't / left / I
5 the / It's / day / coldest / of / year / the
6 than / It's / mine / car / expensive / a / more

3 Find and correct the mistake in each sentence.

1 I speak badly Spanish.
2 He is the more popular footballer in the world; everybody likes him.
3 I had a lot of presents. But the one most I liked was a new bag from my mother.
4 She plays hockey very good.
5 He's ten and he still can't to ride a bike.
6 We are to meeting him at ten o'clock tomorrow.

/12

FUNCTIONAL LANGUAGE

4 Write the missing words.

1 A _____ a wonderful day!
  B Yes, _____ go for a walk in the park.
2 A What are you _____ this afternoon?
  B Nothing. Why?
  A _____ you want to go skateboarding with me?
3 A _____ you like to come to my place for lunch on Saturday?
  B I'd _____ to. Thanks.
4 A _____ what?
  B What?
  A Mum's taking me to London next weekend. I _____ wait!

/8

MY SCORE /30

22–30   10–21   0–9

101

11 FUTURE BODIES

OBJECTIVES

FUNCTIONS:
making predictions; sympathising

GRAMMAR:
will / won't for future predictions; first conditional; time clauses with when / as soon as

VOCABULARY:
parts of the body; expressions with do; when and if

Get TH!NKING

Watch the video and think: how will life be in 100 years?
▶ 31

READING

1. **Label the picture with the words in the list. Write 1–12 in the boxes.**

1 arm	2 bone	3 ear	4 eye	5 finger
6 foot	7 hair	8 leg	9 mouth
10 muscle	11 thumb	12 toe

2. **Write the words from Exercise 1 in the correct column. Some words can go in both columns.**

Body	Face
arm	mouth

3. **SPEAKING** Work in pairs. Discuss the questions.

   Which parts of the body do you use when you:
   - read a book?
   - play football?
   - watch television?
   - make a phone call?
   - eat a meal?
   - walk to school?

   > When you read a book, you use your hands and your eyes.

4. **Look at the picture and the title on page 103. What do you think the article will be about? Choose one of the following.**
   - what we want to look like in the future
   - what the human body will be like in the future
   - how we can change our bodies if we want

5. 🔊 **11.01** Read and listen to the article and check your ideas.

6. **Read the article again and answer the questions.**
   1. What is the most important reason why our bodies will change in the future?
   2. Why will people be taller?
   3. Why will people get weaker?
   4. What will happen to eyes and fingers?
   5. Why will we have one less toe?
   6. Why won't people have so much hair on their bodies?

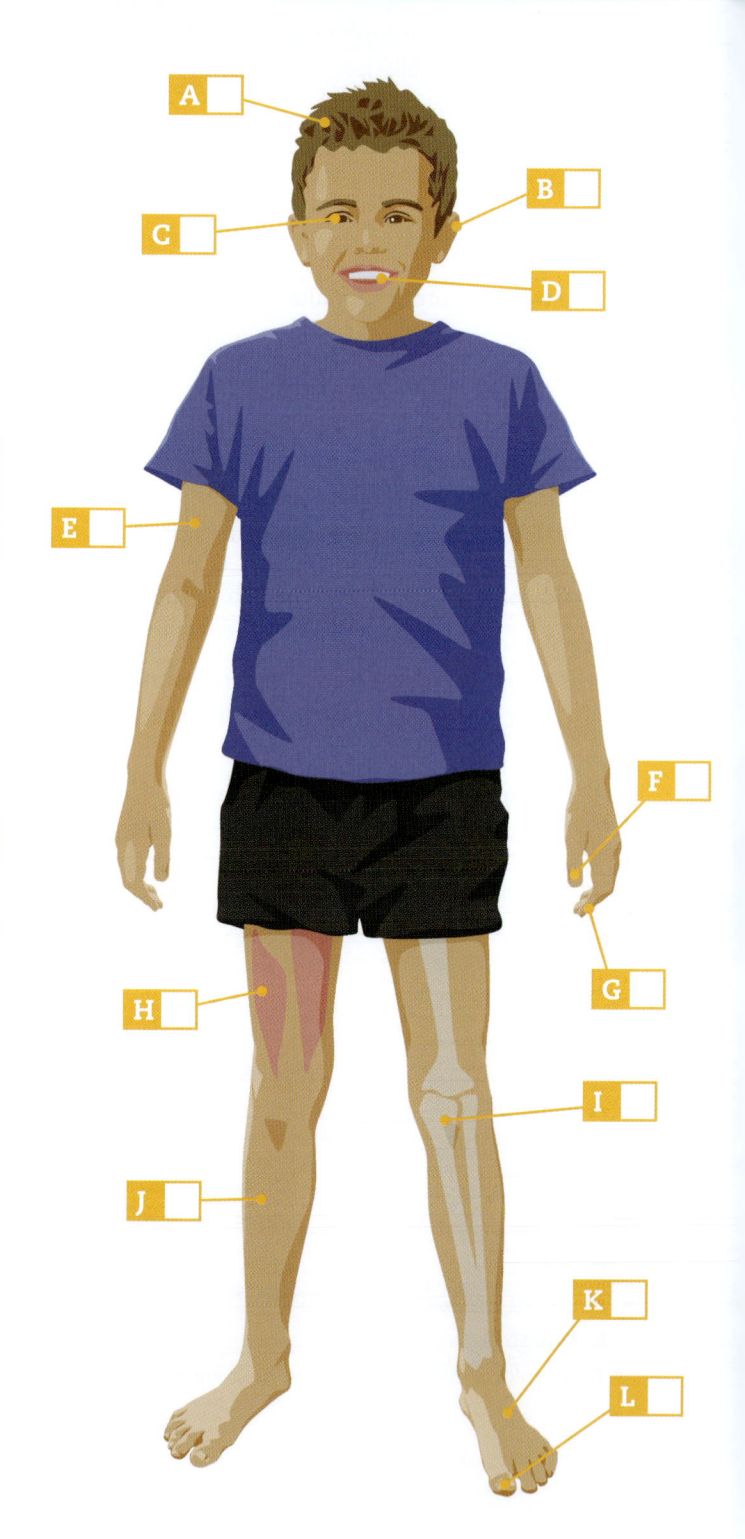

CHANGING BODIES

FUTURE BODIES — UNIT 11

A long time ago, people were very different from the way we are now. For example, if you find a really old house somewhere, you'll see that the doors are usually much lower than they are today. Why? Because hundreds of years ago, people were shorter. Over time, the human body changes to adapt to a new way of life.

Can we expect the human body to change in the future? For sure. And the main reason is that we have more and more technology, and it is changing how we live.

What kind of changes can we expect? Well, no one can be 100 percent sure, but here are some possibilities.

1 Let's start with the example above. Humans are now ten centimetres taller than 150 years ago. So, in the future, people will probably be even taller. Most of us now have much better food than people in the past – and so we grow more.

2 We'll get weaker in more than one way. The most important way is that our muscles will not be as strong as now because we won't do a lot of physical work.

3 We are already using our feet less, and our hands more (think about computers and tablets and so on.) So we can expect that our legs will get shorter and our feet smaller, and at the same time, our fingers will get longer. And our fingers and our eyes will both get better because they'll have to do more work together.

4 Now, what about the mouth? It'll get smaller, perhaps, because technological improvements will mean that we don't need to talk so much – and also because our teeth will get smaller (so mouths don't need to be so big to keep them in).

5 Here's a good one – it's very possible that people will have four toes, not five. The little toe really isn't needed anymore (people who lose them don't miss them), so it will probably disappear sometime in the future.

6 And last but not least – people won't have as much hair on their bodies as now, as we don't need it to keep ourselves warm anymore.

Will all these things happen? And if so, when? These are questions that no one can answer for sure.

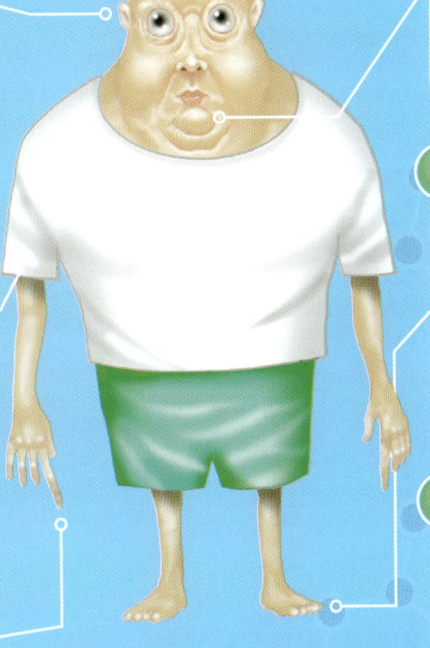

TH!NK values

Exercise and health

7 Read the sentences. Give each one a number from 1 to 5 (1 = doesn't give a lot of importance to health, 5 = gives a lot of importance to health).

1. ☐ You should do regular exercise to make sure your muscles are strong.
2. ☐ It's OK to spend a lot of time sitting in front of the television.
3. ☐ A wonderful thing to do is go for long walks in the fresh air.
4. ☐ Using a computer and writing text messages gives your hands and arms exercise.
5. ☐ You don't have to do sport to be healthy and keep fit.
6. ☐ It's a good idea to do a lot of simple exercise (for example, use the stairs and don't take the lift).

8 SPEAKING Work in small groups. Talk about health and exercise.

1. Together, decide the number that the group is going to give to each of the sentences in Exercise 7.
2. Together, decide on and write another sentence that shows how the group feels about health and exercise.
3. Compare your ideas with other groups.

GRAMMAR
will / won't for future predictions

1 Look at the sentences from the article on page 103. Complete with *will* / *'ll* / *will not* / *won't*. Then complete the rule.

1 Our fingers _____ get longer.
2 They _____ have to do more work together.
3 Our muscles _____ be as strong as now because we _____ do a lot of physical work.

> **RULE:** Use ⁴_____ (*will*) or ⁵_____ (*will not*) + base form of the verb to make predictions about the future.

2 Complete the table.

Positive	Negative
I/you/we/they/he/she/it ¹_____ (will) come.	I/you/we/they/he/she/it ²_____ (will not) come.

Questions	Short answers
³_____ I/you/we/they/he/she/it come?	Yes, I/you/we/they/he/she/it ⁴_____ . No, I/you/we/they/he/she/it ⁵_____ (will not).

3 Complete the conversation. Use *'ll*, *will* or *won't* and a verb from the list.

> be | ~~get~~ | give | go | help | see | stay

Alice Oh, Noah, it's the French test tomorrow! I'm not very good at French. I'm sure I ⁰ **won't get** the answers right!

Noah Don't worry, you ¹_____ fine! You got a good result in your last test.

Alice Yes, but this is more difficult. I really don't feel well. Maybe I ²_____ to school tomorrow. I ³_____ in bed all day.

Noah That ⁴_____ you. The teacher ⁵_____ you the test on Wednesday.

Alice You're right. But what can I do?

Noah Look, why don't I come round to your place this afternoon after school? We can do some French together. You ⁶_____ that it's not so difficult.

Alice Oh, thanks, Noah.

4 **SPEAKING** Work in pairs. Act out the dialogue in Exercise 3.

→ workbook page 100

> **PRONUNCIATION**
> The /h/ consonant sound Go to page 121.

VOCABULARY
Parts of the body

5 Match the words with the photos. Write 1–10 in the boxes.

> 1 ankle | 2 back | 3 elbow | 4 knees | 5 lips | 6 neck | 7 shoulder | 8 stomach | 9 throat | 10 tongue

A B C D E
F G H I J

6 🔊 11.04 Listen and match the speakers with the pictures. Write numbers 1–3 in the boxes.

→ workbook page 102

A B C

FUTURE BODIES UNIT 11

🎧 LISTENING

7 Look at the pictures and say what part of the body each person might have a problem with soon.

A

B

C

8 🔊 11.05 Listen and write the name of the person under each picture.

9 🔊 11.05 Listen again. Mark the statements T (true) or F (false). Correct the false sentences.

1 Lydia thinks she ate too much.
2 Lydia's dad wants her to do the washing-up.
3 The doctor wants Tim to put some ice on his elbow.
4 The doctor thinks the elbow isn't broken.
5 John can't move his neck at all.
6 The doctor agrees with his grandmother.

10 Put the words in order. Who said each of these sentences? (Dad, Doctor, Lydia, Tim)

1 you / Lydia / all / Are / right
2 all / well / at / not / I'm
3 matter / the / with / What's / you
4 got / really / I've / stomach ache / bad / a
5 really / It's / painful
6 it / hurt / Does

ROLE PLAY At the doctor's

Work in pairs. Student A: Go to page 127. Student B: Go to page 128. Take two or three minutes to prepare. Then have a conversation.

WordWise: Expressions with *do*

11 Complete the sentences from page 103.

1 They'll have to do more _____ together.
2 You should do regular _____ to make sure your muscles are strong.
3 You don't have to do _____ to be healthy and keep fit.

12 Complete each sentence with a word from the list.

cooking | homework | ice cream | well

1 Joe's upstairs – he's doing his _____ .
2 Did you do _____ in your exam?
3 They do great _____ at the new café.
4 Mum has a rest on Sundays and we all do the _____ .

13 SPEAKING Complete the questions. Then ask and answer with a partner.

1 _____ you _____ a lot of exercise?
2 Where _____ you _____ your homework?
3 _____ you _____ OK with your homework these days?
4 Who _____ the cleaning in your house?

→ workbook page 102

Look 👁

stomach ache   ear ache   headache   toothache

READING

1 Read the blog quickly. Find a phrase/saying for each of the five pictures.

2 🔊 11.06 Read and listen to the blog. Answer the questions.
1 What is an 'Old Wives' Tale'?
2 Why is it good to eat apples?
3 What did the researchers in New York find out about mothers?
4 What happened to children who ate omega-3 and omega-6?
5 What does the writer think about eating carrots and better night vision?

3 Do you know any more 'Old Wives' Tales'? Tell the class.

Grammar rap! ▶32

GRAMMAR
First conditional

4 Match the sentence halves. Check your answers in the blog. Then complete the rule and the table. Choose the correct words.

1 ☐ If you watch a lot of TV,
2 ☐ If you eat cheese at night,
3 ☐ If you eat fish oil,

a you'll have bad dreams.
b you'll get square eyes.
c it will help to prevent heart problems, too.

> **RULE:** Use the first conditional to talk about ⁴*possible / certain* events and their ⁵*present / future* results.
>
> | *If* clause | Result *clause* |
> |---|---|
> | *If* + present simple, | ⁶_____ (*'ll*) |
> | | ⁷_____ (*won't*) + base form |
>
> It is possible to put the result clause first:
> *If you fall, you'll hurt yourself.* OR
> *You'll hurt yourself if you fall.*

Old Wives' Tales

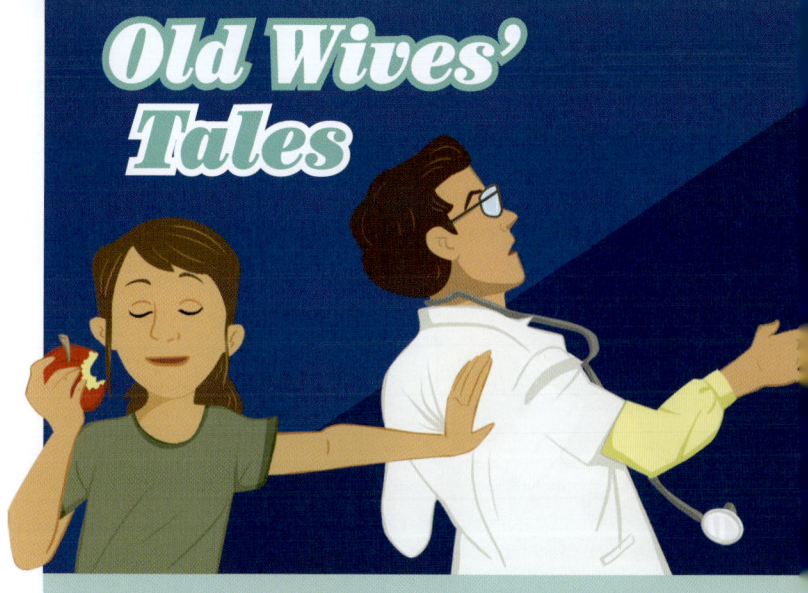

Old Wives' Tales are those 'helpful' things that your grandparents say that are probably not true. They are things like, 'If you watch a lot of TV, you'll get square eyes', 'If you eat carrots, you'll see well in the dark', or 'If you eat cheese at night, you'll have bad dreams'.

But are they nonsense or is there sometimes a little bit of truth in them? We decided to investigate more.

Let's start with a famous one: 'An apple a day keeps the doctor away'. My grandma said this all the time. Well, of course everyone knows that fruit is an important part of a healthy diet. But can one apple really make a difference? A medical study from 2013 says 'yes'. It found that if people over 50 eat an apple a day, their chances of a heart attack are much smaller than people who don't.

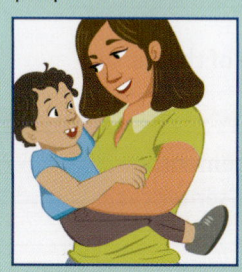

What about 'Gain a child, lose a tooth'? They say that when a woman has a child, a tooth will fall out. Researchers at the New York University College of Dentistry studied more than 2,600 women between the ages of 18 and 64 with one or more children and guess what? They found they had more problems with their teeth than women with no children, although they couldn't say exactly why.

My great uncle was a big believer that 'fish is brain food'. He ate it all the time and he was a clever man, too. It looks like he might be right. Fish have a lot of omega-3 and omega-6 fats in their oil. Some scientists from Oxford studied 120 primary school children, and they discovered that the children who ate omega-3 and omega-6 made big improvements in their schoolwork. If you eat fish oil, it will help to prevent heart problems, too. It seems like eating fish is a good idea.

Finally, what about those carrots? Can they really help your night vision? I've eaten them all my life, but I still walk into things when I get up in the night. Unfortunately, I can't find anything to prove if this is right or wrong. I'll keep looking and I'll let you know as soon as I find out.

FUTURE BODIES UNIT 11

5 Put the words in order to make sentences.

0 see Jane / If / tell / I / I'll / her
  If I see Jane, I'll tell her.
1 my parents / I'm / will / If / late / be angry
2 I / bring it / I'll / to school tomorrow / If / remember
3 you'll / Jake / come / If / you / meet / to the party
4 rain tomorrow / if / the / it / doesn't / We'll / to / beach / go
5 the concert / if / tonight / I / don't / I / won't / feel better / go / to

6 Complete the first conditional sentences with the correct form of the verbs.

0 If Kate _gives_ (give) me some help, I _I'll finish_ (finish) my homework in an hour.
1 You _____ (not meet) anyone if you _____ (not go out).
2 I _____ (come) to your party if my mum _____ (say) I can.
3 If Ken _____ (not want) his ice cream, I _____ (eat) it.
4 Susan _____ (be) angry if she _____ (hear) about this.
5 If we _____ (buy) hamburgers, we _____ (not have) money for the film.

→ workbook page 101

Time clauses with *when* / *as soon as*

7 Read the two sentences and answer the questions. Then complete the rule with *will* and *present simple*.

When a woman has a child, a tooth will fall out.
I'll let you know as soon as I find out.

1 What is the difference between *when* and *as soon as*?
2 Do *has* and *find out* refer to the present or the future?

RULE: In sentences about the future, we use the
³ _____ form after *if* or *when* or *as soon as*, and
⁴ _____ + base form of the verb in the main clause.

8 Complete the sentences. Use the verbs in the list.

arrive | finish (x2) | get (x2)

1 As soon as I _____ my exam results, I'll phone you.
2 When I _____ home, I'll check my messages.
3 The party will start as soon as my friend _____ with the music!
4 When the game _____ , we'll go and have a pizza.
5 I'll lend you the book as soon as I _____ reading it.

→ workbook page 101

VOCABULARY
when and *if*

9 Match sentences 1 and 2 with the explanations.

1 **When I see Martin**, I'll give him your message.
2 **If I see Martin**, I'll give him your message.

a It is possible that I will meet Martin.
b I know that I will meet Martin.

10 Complete the sentences with *if* or *when*.

0 I can't talk to you now. I'll phone you _when_ I get home.
1 A What are you doing tomorrow?
  B _____ there's a good film on, I'll probably go to the cinema.
2 I'm not sure if I want to go to the party tonight. But _____ I decide to go, I'll phone you.
3 It's too hot to go for a walk now. Let's go out in the evening _____ it's cooler.
4 You can watch some TV _____ you finish your homework, and not before!
5 It's the football final tonight. I'll be very happy _____ my team wins.

→ workbook page 102

LISTENING AND WRITING
A phone message

11 Which of these things do you NOT need to write down if you take a phone message? Mark them with a cross (*X*).

1 the name of the caller ☐
2 the telephone number of the person who takes the message ☐
3 the name of the person who the message is for ☐
4 the telephone number of the caller ☐
5 what the caller wants ☐

12 🔊 11.07 Listen to a telephone conversation. Complete the message.

Message from: ¹_____
For: ²_____
Message: she needs ³_____ .
Please ⁴_____
Number to call: ⁵_____

DEVELOPING SPEAKING

1 🔊 **11.08** Look at the photo. What happened? Where is she now? Listen and read to check.

Luke: Jessica, hi. Oh no! What happened to you?

Jessica: Hi, Luke. Oh, it's so silly. Yesterday, I slipped and fell on the stairs at home. It was my own fault, of course. I mean, I was looking at my phone and not looking where I was going. And now look. A broken leg.

Luke: Poor you! You're lucky it wasn't worse than that.

Jessica: I know, you're right. But I'm so disappointed. And angry, too. It's our cup final match on Saturday, and now I can't play.

Luke: That's a shame. But hey, don't be so hard on yourself. Everyone makes mistakes now and again.

Jessica: I suppose so. But I'm really upset about it anyway.

Luke: Listen. I've got an idea. Can you wait here for a minute or two?

Jessica: Sure. Whatever. But what are you going to do?

Luke: Wait and see!

two minutes later …

Luke: Right, done, all fixed. How about watching the FA Cup semi-final on Sunday? You know, the match in London. Wembley.

Jessica: What, on TV somewhere?

Luke: No, the real thing. My dad won three tickets to go and see it. He says he can give me two. So how about it? Want to go with us?

Jessica: Seriously? Luke, that's brilliant! I can't wait! Thank you so much!

Luke: No problem. Tell you what, though.

Jessica: What?

Luke: When we go into the stadium, don't start looking at your phone, OK? I don't want you to fall again and break your other leg!

2 🔊 **11.08** Read and listen again. Correct the wrong information.

1 Jessica slipped when she was looking at a book.
2 Now she can't play in the final game on Sunday.
3 They are going to watch the game on TV.
4 Luke is getting three tickets from his father.

Phrases for fluency

3 Find the expressions 1–6 in the dialogue. Who says them? Match them to the definitions a–f.

1 I mean, …
2 I suppose so.
3 Whatever.
4 Wait and see.
5 I can't wait!
6 Tell you what …

a What I want to say is …
b I really don't care.
c Here's what I think …
d I think that's possibly true.
e You'll know in the future.
f I'm excited about a future event.

4 Complete the mini-dialogues with expressions in Exercise 3.

1 **A** I'm going to see a film on Saturday! _____ !
   B _____ – we could go together. _____ , if that's OK with you.
2 **A** What are you going to give me for my birthday?
   B It's a surprise! _____ .
3 **A** Do you want to go out or stay at home?
   B _____ , Alex.
4 **A** Can I go out tonight, Dad?
   B _____ . But don't be late back, OK?

⚙️ FUNCTIONS
Sympathising

> **KEY LANGUAGE**
> I'm sorry to hear that.
> Poor thing (him / her / John / Sally, etc).
> That's a shame.
> Poor you.

5 Complete the mini-dialogues using phrases from the Key Language box.

1 **Jessica** Now look! A broken arm!
   Luke _____ .
2 **Jessica** It's our big match on Saturday, and now I can't play.
   Luke _____ .
3 **Luke** Jim, have you heard about Jessica? She broke her arm!
   Jim Really? _____ .
4 **Molly** My granny's very ill.
   Steve _____ her.

6 Read the situations. What can you say in each one?

1 You meet a friend. You know that your friend lost something important yesterday.   *Poor you!*
2 You hear that someone stole Tim's bike last weekend. You meet Tim's brother.
3 A neighbour says: 'I feel terrible today. I'm ill.'
4 Your friends say they can't come to your party.

LIFE COMPETENCIES

We all have negative feelings sometimes, and it's easy to do or say bad things when we feel like this. Learning what to do when we have negative feelings helps us not make situations worse, or hurt other people and their feelings.

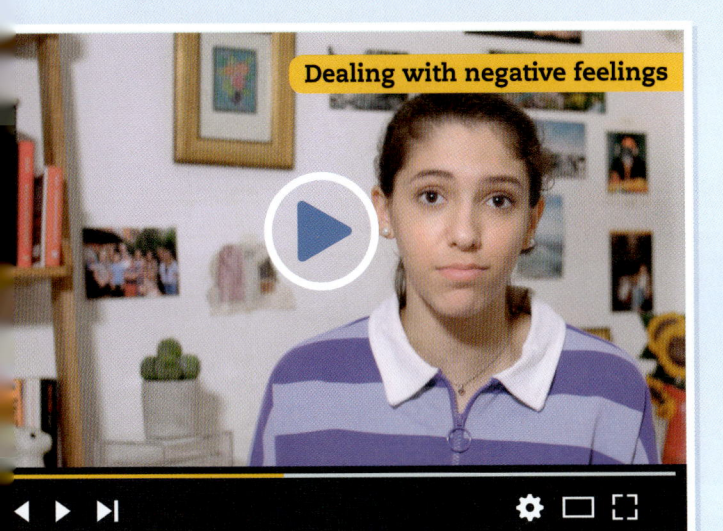

Dealing with negative feelings

1 ▶ 33 Watch the video. How does she make herself feel better?

2 ▶ 33 Watch again and answer the questions.

> 1 Which family members make her feel negative?
> 2 What does Ben do?
> 3 What are three other things that made her feel unhappy this week?
> 4 What are two solutions she mentions for dealing with negative feelings?
> 5 What does she enjoy doing?

3 Anger is an example of a negative feeling. Read James's story. Why were his parents angry with him?

4 **SPEAKING** Work in pairs. Discuss these questions.

1 What did Alex do to James?
2 How did James feel?
3 What did James do?
4 How did James feel after this?

5 James threw the book because he was angry with his brother. Which of these actions do you think James should do when he feels angry with his brother in the future?

> drink water | throw something bigger
> go to his bedroom and sit quietly | shout
> speak to his mum or dad | count to 100
> go for a walk/run | cry

6 Can you think of more good actions to do when you're angry?

Me and my world

7 **SPEAKING** Think of three things for each list. Then compare with a partner.

a things that make me feel negative
b things I do when I'm feeling negative
c things I should do when I'm feeling negative

TIPS FOR DEALING WITH NEGATIVE FEELINGS

- Don't react to a bad situation when you are angry about it. Take a break and think calmly about how to react.
- Talk to others. It can help to get a different perspective from a friend.
- If you react badly, learn from it. Think about how you can react differently next time.

My brother, Alex, and I are good friends most of the time. He's only a year older than me, so we like a lot of the same things and share a lot of friends. Sometimes, though, like most brothers, we fight and it can get quite bad.

Fights often start when we're playing computer games. We both like winning, especially when our friends are with us.

Two months ago, we had a really big fight. I was nervous because I had a violin exam the next week, and so I was practising for an hour or two every day. When I practise, I have to wear my glasses. I wear them for any type of reading or computer work, so it's not strange for Alex to see me wearing them.

Anyway, one day, Alex started calling me 'four-eyes'. At first, I just didn't listen, but after two days, it started to annoy me and I told him to stop. He started laughing and dancing and singing 'Four-eyes! Four-eyes!' I was so angry and wanted him to stop, so I picked up a book that was on the table and threw it at him.

As soon as the book hit Alex in the face, I knew it was bad. Alex and Mum spent six hours at the hospital. Alex's nose was broken. I felt terrible. He didn't speak to me for a week, but Mum and Dad had a lot to say to me.

12 TRAVEL THE WORLD

OBJECTIVES

FUNCTIONS:
talking about travel and transport; talking about life experiences

GRAMMAR:
present perfect simple; present perfect with *ever* / *never*; present perfect vs. past simple

VOCABULARY:
transport and travel; travel verbs

Get TH!NKING

Watch the video and think: is travelling just for tourists?

▶ 34

A B C D E F

READING

1 Match the words with the photos. Write 1–6 in the boxes.

> 1 bicycle | 2 boat | 3 bus
> 4 car | 5 plane | 6 train

2 **SPEAKING** Work in pairs. Ask and answer the questions.

How do you travel …
- to school?
- to the cinema?
- to the shops?
- when you go on holiday?

I usually go by bike.

I often take the bus.

3 **SPEAKING** Work in pairs or small groups. Which type of transport is:
- cheap?
- dangerous?
- expensive?
- boring?
- exciting?
- your favourite?

4 Look at the photos and the title of the article on page 111. What do you think the article is about? Choose one of the following:
- someone who travels a lot for work
- someone who runs very quickly
- someone who travels more than anyone else

5 🔊 12.01 Read and listen to the article to check.

6 Read the article again. Correct the information in these sentences.

1 Cassie used one passport to travel round the world.
2 She didn't break the old record by very much.
3 She left her job because she had enough money.
4 Sometimes she didn't go running because she was too tired.
5 She talked to tourists about how tourism can help countries.
6 She tried to find her American ancestors in different countries.
7 She's tired now and doesn't want to travel anymore.
8 She wants to travel to Antarctica for the first time.

110

TRAVEL THE WORLD UNIT 12

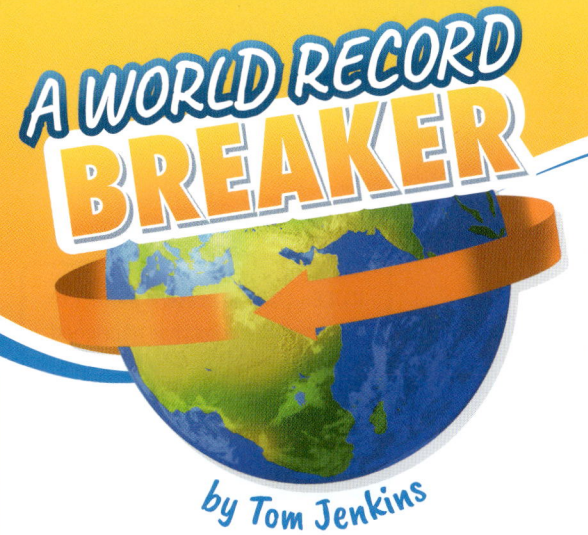

A WORLD RECORD BREAKER

by Tom Jenkins

She's taken over 255 flights. She's filled five passports, she's planted trees, has spoken to students in over 40 different countries, and she's funded all $110,000 through sponsors and investors. Now, her amazing adventure has finished and 29-year-old Cassie De Pecol has done it: she's broken two Guinness World records. After 18 months and 10 days, Cassie has become the fastest person to visit every country in the world, and the first woman on record to do so, in half the old record time.

Back in 2014, Cassie decided to leave her job because she wasn't doing what she really wanted to do. What she really wanted to do was to see the world, and she started making plans for her great journey. She started saving all the money she could, and in July 2015, she left home to start her travels. Just over a year and a half later, on 2 February 2017, she arrived in Yemen, the 196th and last country on her (very!) long list.

Of course, she didn't have much time to see each country, but she made sure to use her time well. She spent an average of two to five days in each country. The best parts of her journey included: meeting local people, travelling to remote places on her own, planting trees and educating students on important world issues. Cassie is a keen runner and triathlete and so she also didn't enjoy staying in places where she didn't feel safe enough to go for a run.

But Cassie's journey was not just one long holiday. She also wanted to make a difference. She went as a Peace Ambassador (a special representative) for the International Institute for Peace Through Tourism. In many of the countries she went to, she met and talked to local students – they discussed how tourism can be used to help each country. Cassie is also very worried about the environment, so she agreed to help another organisation called Adventurers and Scientists for Conservation, funded by National Geographic. In many of the countries she went to, she collected samples of water for them to test for the presence of microplastics.

Cassie has always wanted to travel. When she was at school, she had a strong interest in other cultures. She was curious about how Americans have their origins in countries all over the world, and she wanted to find out more about where their ancestors came from. This journey was a chance to start answering some of these questions. So, has she finished her travels now? No, she hasn't – not at all! Cassie hasn't become tired of travelling, and she is already making plans for her next journey. And she didn't forget Antarctica! She visited it on the last stop of her expedition.

TH!NK values

Travel broadens the mind

7 Read what people said about Cassie De Pecol. Match the comments (1–4) with the values (a–d).

1 ☐ She's been to every country, so I think she probably understands all kinds of people.
2 ☐ She's probably a better person now because she's learned so many things.
3 ☐ I think it's wonderful that she was an ambassador for Peace Through Tourism.
4 ☐ She wanted to find ancestors, so she's interested in her past and other people's.

a helping to make the world a better place
b self-improvement
c learning about history around the world
d learning about other cultures

8 **SPEAKING** How important are the values in Exercise 9 for you? Put them in order from 1–4. Compare your ideas in class. Say why you think the values are important or not.

GRAMMAR
Present perfect simple

1 **Complete the sentences from the article on page 111. Then complete the rule.**
   1 She _____ to students in over 40 different countries.
   2 She _____ two Guinness World records.
   3 Cassie _____ always _____ to travel.
   4 _____ she _____ her travels now? No, she _____ .
   5 Cassie _____ tired of travelling.

   RULE: Use the present perfect to talk about actions that happened sometime in your life up to now. Form the present perfect with the present simple form of ⁶_____ + past participle.

2 **Find other examples of the present perfect in the article on page 111.**

3 **Complete the table.**

Positive	Negative	Questions	Short answers
I/you/we/they 've (¹_____) worked.	I/you/we/they haven't (have not) worked.	⁴_____ I/you/we/they worked?	Yes, I/you/we/they ⁶_____ . No, I/you/we/they haven't.
He/she/it 's (²_____) worked.	He/she/it hasn't (³_____) worked.	⁵_____ he/she/it worked?	Yes, he/she/it has. No, he/she/it ⁷_____ .

4 **Complete the past participles. Use the irregular verbs list on page 128 of the Workbook to help you.**

base form	past participle
0 be	been
1 do	_____
2 go	_____
3 see	_____
4 write	_____
5 meet	_____

base form	past participle
6 speak	_____
7 eat	_____
8 take	_____
9 fly	_____
10 swim	_____
11 win	_____

Look
1 She **has gone** to New York. = She is not here now – she is in New York.
2 She **has been** to New York. = She went to New York and came back (at some time in the past).

5 **Jack and Diane are 25 years old. When they were teenagers, they wanted to do many things – and they have done some of them but not all of them. Look at the table. Complete the sentences about them.**

	learn French	visit Paris	write a book	work in the US	make a lot of money
Diane	✓	✗	✓	✓	✗
Jack	✓	✓	✗	✗	✗

0 Jack and Diane _____have learned_____ French.
1 Diane _____ Paris.
2 Diane _____ a book.
3 Jack _____ Paris.
4 Jack _____ in the US.
5 They _____ a lot of money.

6 **WRITING Look at the information about Sue and Harry. Write sentences about them.**

	visit another country	fly in a plane	swim in the sea	touch a snake	take a driving test
Sue	✓	✗	✗	✗	✓
Harry	✓	✓	✗	✓	✗

7 **SPEAKING Work in pairs. Say things about yourself and people you know. Remember: don't say when in the past.**

My mother has lived in Africa.
I've won two tennis competitions.

→ workbook page 108

112

TRAVEL THE WORLD UNIT 12

LISTENING

8 🔊 12.02 Richard Ward is on a radio programme. Listen and choose the correct answers.

1 Richard is talking about *travelling well / the dangers of travelling*.
2 Richard thinks it's important to *go to famous places / go to places other people don't go*.
3 Richard always takes a scarf with him because *he goes to cold places / he can use it in many different ways*.

9 🔊 12.02 Listen again and answer the questions.

1 When he came home from travelling, where did he stay?
2 How many books has he written?
3 What, for Richard, is the difference between a tourist and a traveller?
4 Why is it good to get lost?
5 What are three things you can do with a scarf?

Grammar rap! ▶35

GRAMMAR
Present perfect with *ever / never*

10 Complete the sentences with *ever* or *never* and complete the rule.

1 Have you _____ got lost?
2 I've _____ had my own home.

> **RULE:** When we use the present perfect to talk about experiences and we want to say:
> • 'at no time in (my) life' we use the word ³_____
> • 'at any time in (your) life' we use the word ⁴_____
> The words *ever* and *never* usually come between *have* and the past participle.

11 Complete the mini-dialogues with the words in the list.

| been | eaten | ever | have |
| never | no | played | yes |

1 A Have you _____ watched a silent film?
  B Yes, I _____ .
2 A Have you ever _____ to the Olympic Games?
  B _____ , I've never been to them.
3 A Have you ever _____ tennis?
  B _____ , I have.
4 A Have you ever _____ a really hot curry?
  B No, I've _____ tried curry.

→ workbook page 109

FUNCTIONS
Talking about life experiences

12 Work in pairs. Ask and answer the questions.

1 ever / see / a snake?
2 ever / eat / something horrible?
3 ever / be / on television?
4 ever / speak / to someone from the US?
5 ever / win / a prize?
6 ever / be / to another country?

> Have you ever seen a snake?
> Yes, I have. It was a python at the zoo.
> No, I haven't.

SPEAKING

13 Work in pairs. Think of a famous person. Ask about things that the famous person has done in their life and imagine the answers. Use some of the verbs in the list.

| drive | eat | play | see |
| stay | travel | win | write |

> Mr President – have you ever eaten fried spiders?
> Yes, I have. I eat them all the time.

Train to TH!NK

Exploring differences

14 SPEAKING Work in small groups. Look at the pairs of things. Answer the questions.

a What is the same?
b What is different?

1 A car and a taxi
2 A train and a plane
3 A holiday and a journey
4 A tourist and a traveller

The same: a car and a taxi have wheels / doors / a driver.
Different: you drive your car, but a taxi driver drives the taxi. In a taxi, you have to pay.

15 SPEAKING Compare your ideas with others in the class.

> **PRONUNCIATION**
> Sentence stress Go to page 121. 🎧

TRAVELLING THE WORLD FROM YOUR SOFA!

Seventeen-year-old Tom Davidson hasn't left his home since he was 15. The last time he went out was two years ago. He was walking to catch a bus when he was hit on the head by a sign falling from a building. He spent more than two months in hospital and doctors told him he was lucky to be alive. The accident left Tom with agoraphobia: the idea of being outdoors makes him feel extremely anxious.

The problem is that Tom loves travelling. Before his accident, Tom spent most weekends exploring his home city of London by bus, underground train and his scooter, and he looked forward to holidays abroad with his parents. Now the idea of driving in a car to France or taking a plane to Italy terrifies him.

However, there is a way that Tom can still visit the most remote corners of the world without leaving the security of his home: Google Maps. In the last year and a half, Tom has visited every country in the world where Google Maps has been and taken photos. Using 'street view', he has walked down the streets of the world's most famous cities, he has seen all the world's most amazing geographical features and he has visited places in the world that he didn't know existed: all of this from the comfort of his home.

Tom's virtual travel is more than just a hobby – it has become an art project. He has taken more than 5,000 screenshots of places he has visited and last week, there was an exhibition of his best photos at a school near his home (but of course, he didn't go). Tom also hopes that his online journeys will help him eventually to overcome his agoraphobia. As he discovers more places that he wants to visit one day, he is becoming more and more determined to leave his home. And his dream, if he can, is to work in the travel industry, for example as a flight attendant or a tour guide.

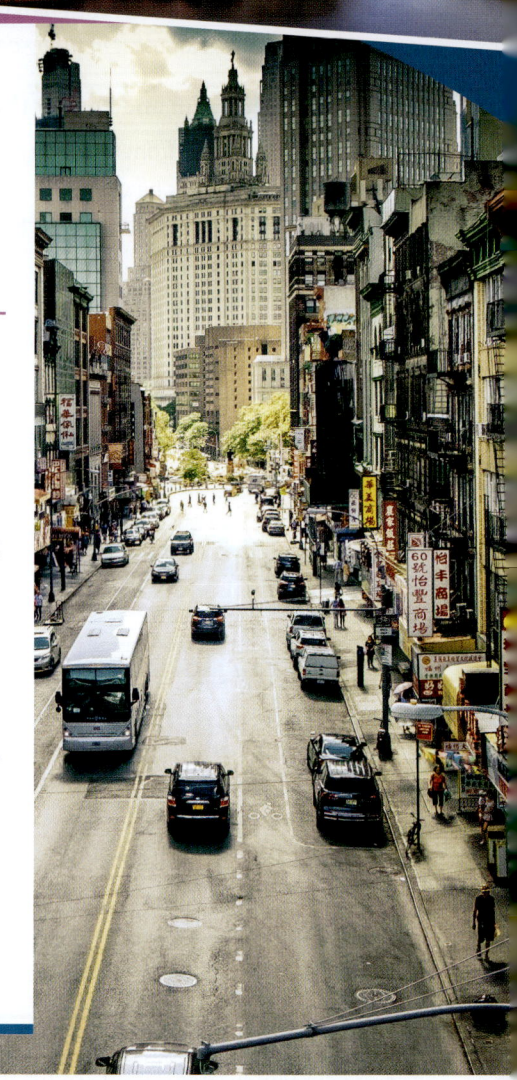

READING

1 Read the text quickly. Find out:
- what problem Tom has got
- what he uses to 'travel'
- what his dream for the future is

2 **12.05** Read and listen to the text. Correct the wrong information.
1 Tom hasn't left his home for three years.
2 His agoraphobia started when he was hit by a car.
3 Before the accident, he often went on holiday with his parents in London.
4 Using Google Maps, he has visited every country in the world.
5 Tom uses 'street view' to go to places that he knows about.
6 Tom hopes that in the future he can get a job with Google Maps.

3 **SPEAKING** Work in two groups. Group A: you are tour guides. Group B: you are flight attendants. In your group, think of answers to these questions.
1 When did you start your job?
2 Tell us about a problem you've had.
3 Tell us about a funny moment you've had.
4 Do you like your job or do you want to change?

4 **SPEAKING** Work in pairs – one student from Group A with one student from Group B. Ask and answer the questions.

5 **SPEAKING** Decide whose answers were best: the tour guide's or the flight attendant's.

TRAVEL THE WORLD UNIT 12

GRAMMAR
Present perfect vs. past simple

6 Complete the sentences from the article on page 114. Complete the rule with the names of the tenses.

1 The last time he _____ out was two years ago.
2 He _____ down the streets of the world's most famous cities.
3 Before his accident, Tom _____ most weekends exploring his home city of London.
4 He _____ more than 5,000 screenshots.
5 Tom's virtual travel is more than just a hobby – it _____ an art project.
6 Last week, there _____ an exhibition of his best photos at a school near his home.

RULE: Use the ⁷_____ to talk about situations or actions at a particular time in the past. Use the ⁸_____ to talk about situations or actions in the past, when we don't say when they happened.

7 Find more examples of verbs in the past simple and present perfect in the article on page 114.

8 Choose the correct forms.

My name's Michael Edwards and I'm 26.
¹*I've been / I was* very lucky in my life because I have a good job and I travel a lot for work.
²*I've lived / I lived* in three different countries: Thailand, India and Singapore.
³*I've lived / I lived* in Singapore from 2017 to 2019. I live in Thailand now.
⁴*I've got / I got* married two years ago. My wife and I travel a lot together and ⁵*we've seen / we saw* some wonderful places. Last year, ⁶*we've seen / we saw* the Taj Mahal in India.
⁷*I've done / I did* some crazy things in my life, but the craziest was last month –
⁸*I've gone / I went* by minibus all the way to the north of Thailand. ⁹*It's been / It was* really exciting!

→ workbook page 109

VOCABULARY
Transport and travel

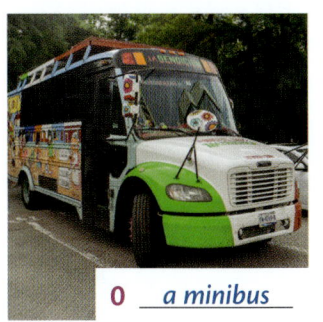

9 🔊 12.06 Write the words under the photos. Listen and check.

a minibus | a helicopter | a tram | a motorbike
a scooter | an underground train

Travel verbs

10 Complete the sentences with the correct form of the verbs in the list.

catch | drive | fly | miss | ride | take

0 I had to walk home because I **missed** the bus.
1 I ran very fast, but I didn't _____ the train.
2 I have never _____ in a helicopter.
3 My brother's got a motorbike and now he's learning to _____ it.
4 We got in the car and we _____ to France.
5 The rain was terrible, so we _____ a taxi.

11 **SPEAKING** Work in pairs. Ask each other questions. Use the verbs in Exercise 10 and the forms of transport you can see on this page and page 110.

Have you ever flown in a helicopter?

No, I haven't. Have you ever taken a tram?

Yes, I took a tram in Lisbon when I was on holiday.

→ workbook page 110

0 a minibus
1 _____
2 _____
3 _____
4 _____
5 _____

115

Culture

TH!NK — Hard journeys for schoolchildren

1. Look at the photos and answer the questions. Then say what you think the article is going to be about.

   Where can you see …
   - a student riding to school on a donkey?
   - children walking to school along some rail tracks?

2. 🔊 12.07 Read and listen to the article and say which country each photo is from.

HARD JOURNEYS FOR SCHOOLCHILDREN

'How do you get to school?' This question often gets an answer like 'By bus' or 'I walk' or 'My parents take me by car'. But not always – there are children in many different parts of the world who, every day, have to go on a difficult journey in order to get to their lessons. They travel for kilometres on foot, or by boat, bicycle, donkey or train. They cross deserts, mountains, rivers, snow and ice: for example, the children of the Iñupiat community in Alaska go to school and then come back when it is dark, in extremely cold temperatures. And they are not the only ones. Kids in many countries do this and more.

These children in Indonesia have to cross a bridge ten metres above a dangerous river to get to their class on time. (Some years ago the bridge fell down after very heavy rain.) Then they walk many more kilometres through the forest to their school in Banten.

A pupil at Gulu Village Primary School, China, rides a donkey as his grandfather walks beside him. Gulu is a mountain village in a national park. The school is far away from the village. It is halfway up a mountain, so it takes five hours to climb from the bottom of the mountain to the school. The children have a dangerous journey: the path is only 45 centimetres wide in some places.

In Sri Lanka, some children have to cross a piece of wood between two walls of an old castle every morning. Their teacher watches them carefully. But in Galle, Sri Lanka, many girls don't go to school – they have to go to work or get married young. So girls are happy to take a risk in order to get to school.

Six-year-old Fabricio Oliveira gets on his donkey every morning to ride with his friends for over an hour through a desert region in the very dry Sertão area of northeast Brazil. Their school is in Extrema. It's a tiny village – very few people live there.

These children live in houses on Chetla Road in Delhi, India. Their homes are near the busy and dangerous railway lines that go to Alipur station. Every morning they walk along the tracks to get to their school, 40 minutes away.

So one question we can ask is: why do the children do this? Because their parents make them do it? The answer, in many cases, is no – it's because for them going to school means a better future: they hope to get a job and money so they can help their families and their neighbours. And this is why rivers, deserts or danger won't stop them on their way to school.

TRAVEL THE WORLD UNIT 12

3 Read the article again. What difficulties do children in these places face to get to school?

1. the children of the Iñupiat community in Alaska
2. the children who go to the school in Banten, Indonesia
3. the children who go to Gulu Village Primary School, China
4. the children who go to school in Galle, Sri Lanka
5. fabricio Oliveira in Brazil
6. the children who live along Chetla Road in Delhi, India

4 VOCABULARY There are eight highlighted words in the article. Match the words with these meanings. Write the words.

0	from one side to the other	wide
1	people living in houses near you	_____
2	a trip	_____
3	do something that can be dangerous	_____
4	a group of houses usually in the countryside	_____
5	the things that trains move on	_____
6	very, very small	_____
7	not late	_____

5 SPEAKING Which journey do you think is the most difficult? Compare with others in the class.

WRITING
Someone I admire

1 INPUT Read Javed's essay about 'Someone I admire'. Answer the questions.

1. When and where was his aunt Priti born?
2. Where does she live now and when did she move there?
3. How does she travel in her work?
4. What does she want to do in the future?
5. Why does Javed admire his aunt?

2 Find examples in the essay of the word *in* with these things.

1. a year
2. a month
3. a city
4. a country

3 ANALYSE Look at the four paragraphs of Javed's essay about his aunt. Match the paragraphs with the contents.

Paragraph 1	a	what she does and how
Paragraph 2	b	why he admires her
Paragraph 3	c	when and where she was born
Paragraph 4	d	why she does these things

Someone I admire

(1) My Aunt Priti is a really great woman. She was born in England in 1980, in a city called Leicester, but now she lives and works in Angola. She went to Angola in 2014.

(2) My aunt is a doctor and she worked at a hospital in Birmingham for a few years. But in 2014, she decided to go and work in small villages in Angola because she heard that they needed doctors. She travels from village to village to help people. She has a small car that she uses. Sometimes, though, she goes in a very small plane because the roads aren't good enough.

(3) Aunt Priti says that she wants to stay there because there is a lot of work to do. She has also met a man there – she told me in an email that they are getting married in July next year. Aunt Priti hopes that she can help to teach Angolan people to become doctors in the future. She has learned a lot of Portuguese there, too – that can't be easy!

(4) I said before that she's a great woman. Why do I think that? Well, because she is helping other people and is happy doing that, and because she has learned a lot about another culture.

4 PLAN Think of someone that you admire: a famous person; or someone you know in your own life; or someone you invent.

For the person, think about:
- facts about their life (when they were born, etc.)
- what they do, where and how, when they started
- what they want to do in the future
- why you admire them

5 PRODUCE Write an essay called 'Someone I admire' in about 150 words. Use the example essay and language above to help you.

117

A2 Key for Schools

READING AND WRITING
Part 3: 3-option multiple choice
→ workbook page 115

1 For each question, choose the correct answer.

Hotels in Sydney, Australia

The Green Hotel (7/10)

Place
The Green Hotel is downtown and is walking distance to many restaurants, cafés and shops. It's a long way from the airport. It's also on a busy road, but you don't hear traffic noise in the rooms (but noise from other guests can be a problem at night). There aren't any really good views from the hotel, but the garden at the back is nice.

Style & character
The hotel is popular, mostly with young people, so you can meet other travellers. The staff are pleasant, helpful and of course speak English and one or two other languages, too. It's a clean place and there's a sitting room for guests to sit and talk in.

Rooms
Some rooms have a bathroom, and of course they're the best. All the rooms are quite small, but have a table and a reading lamp. See above about noise. The beds are small but comfortable and everything is very clean.

Food
The only meal you can have at the hotel is breakfast. It's included in the price and not at all bad. There is a good choice of fruit, cheese, cereals and bread. Eggs are freshly cooked for a small extra charge.

Value for money
For people who can't pay high prices, this is a good choice. Room prices are quite cheap. At popular times of the year (October to January) there is a minimum three-night stay. Check the website for more details.

1 Where is The Green Hotel?
   A It isn't far from the airport.
   B It is near the city centre.
   C It is opposite a large garden.

2 Guests at the hotel
   A speak many different languages.
   B can sit in the sitting room to talk.
   C are usually old people.

3 In the rooms,
   A you can hear other guests.
   B there's always a bathroom.
   C the beds are all large.

4 What does the article say about breakfast?
   A It's expensive.
   B It's pretty good.
   C It's very bad.

5 What does the article say about prices?
   A The hotel is more expensive in the high season.
   B Guests pay more if they only stay for two nights.
   C The rooms don't cost very much all year long.

Part 5: Open cloze
→ workbook page 97

2 For each question, write the correct answer.
Write **one** word for each gap.

Hey!
For today's blog, I'm going ⁰ _to_ talk about my next trip. I love travelling and seeing different cultures. So far, I've ¹_____ to 56 countries. Next year, if I have enough money, I'm going to buy ²_____ aeroplane ticket and visit Thailand.
I'm excited about this journey. I've ³_____ been to Asia before. First, I'm going to ⁴_____ to Bangkok from my home, Sydney. When I arrive, I'm going to take a taxi to my aunt's house. ⁵_____ my plan goes well, I will travel through Thailand on the Chao Phraya River by ⁶_____ .

LISTENING
Part 5: Matching
→ workbook page 61

3 🔊 12.08 For each question, choose the correct answer.

You will hear Jack talking to a friend about his transport project. How does each person get to school?

Example
0 Jack   E   E on foot

People   **Transport**
                           A bike
1 Olivia ☐   B boat
2 Rashid ☐   C bus
3 Morris ☐   D car
4 Leslie ☐   E on foot
5 Adam ☐   F scooter
                           G taxi
                           H train

TEST YOURSELF

UNITS 11 & 12

VOCABULARY

1 Complete the sentences with the words in the list. There are two extra words.

> back | caught | flew | helicopter | lip | missed | neck | ride | scooter | stomach ache | tongue | trams

1 He's really rich. He goes to work by _____ and he lands on the roof of his office building.
2 I've got a _____ . I think I ate something bad for lunch.
3 We _____ the last train home, so we walked home.
4 Open your mouth. I want to take a look at your _____ .
5 I can't _____ a motorbike, but I really want to learn how to. I think they're great.
6 I fell and cut my mouth and made my top _____ bleed.
7 My dad rides his _____ to work. It's quicker than going by car and a lot cheaper.
8 We _____ over the sea and the beaches in a small plane. The views were fantastic!
9 I never sleep on my _____ .
10 Many cities are now using _____ to get people to and from work.

/10

GRAMMAR

2 Put the words in order to make sentences.

1 phone / I'll / home / you / get / soon / as / I / as
2 taxi / I / train / miss / if / the / take / a / I'll
3 ever / Have / Argentina / you / been / to
4 seen / She's / sea / never / the
5 different / six / lived / cities / in / They've
6 grandchildren / be / easy / for / won't / our / Life

3 Find and correct the mistake in each sentence.

1 She's played volleyball yesterday.
2 If we will be late, the teacher will be angry.
3 I have ever broken an arm or a leg.
4 I've never gone to Japan.
5 She has took a lot of photos on holiday.
6 One day in the future people will living on the moon.

/12

FUNCTIONAL LANGUAGE

4 Write the missing words.

1 A What's the _____ ?
  B My back _____ a lot.
2 A I've _____ a headache.
  B I'm sorry to _____ that. Would you like some medicine?
3 A Have you _____ been to France?
  B No, I _____ .
4 A Do you think it _____ rain this afternoon?
  B I don't know. I'm not _____ .

/8

MY SCORE /30

22–30 😊   10–21 😐   0–9 😒

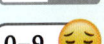

119

PRONUNCIATION

UNIT 1
/s/, /z/, /ɪz/ sounds

1. 🔊 **1.02** Listen to the sentences.

   Gus make**s** cake**s** and sweet**s**. He work**s** hard and sleep**s** a lot.

   Jame**s** enjoy**s** all kind**s** of game**s**. He play**s** a lot of football with his friend**s**.

   Liz**'s** job is fun. She wash**es** and brush**es** hors**es** and relax**es** by riding them.

2. Say the words with the /s/, /z/ and /ɪz/ endings.

3. 🔊 **1.03** Listen and repeat. Then practise with a partner.

UNIT 2
Contractions

1. 🔊 **2.05** Listen to the dialogue.

   Tom   **Here's** your pizza, Jane.
   Jane   **That's** not my pizza. I **don't** like cheese.
   Tom   But Jane! **They've** all got cheese!
   Jane   No, they **haven't**. **There's** one without it.
   Tom   **You're** right … **it's** this one. Here you are.

2. Say the words in blue.

3. 🔊 **2.06** Listen and repeat. Then practise with a partner.

UNIT 3
Vowel sounds /ɪ/ and /iː/

1. 🔊 **3.06** Listen to the tongue twisters.

   J**i**ll w**i**shes sh**e** had f**i**sh and ch**i**ps for d**i**nner.
   P**e**te's **ea**ting m**ea**t with ch**ee**se and p**ea**s.
   P**e**te and J**i**ll drink t**ea** with m**i**lk.

2. Say the words with the short /ɪ/ sound. Say the words with the long /iː/ sound.

3. 🔊 **3.07** Listen and repeat. Then practise with a partner.

UNIT 4
-er /ə/ at the end of words

1. 🔊 **4.03** Listen to the tongue twister.

   Jennif**er**'s fath**er**'s a firefight**er**,
   Oliv**er**'s moth**er**'s a travel writ**er**,
   Pet**er**'s sist**er**'s a lorry driv**er**,
   And Amb**er**'s broth**er**'s a deep-sea div**er**.

2. Say the words with the weak -er sound (the schwa /ə/).

3. 🔊 **4.04** Listen and repeat. Then practise with a partner.

UNIT 5
Regular past tense endings: /d/, /t/ and /ɪd/

1. 🔊 **5.03** Listen to the dialogue.

   Mum   What happen**ed** in the kitchen, Jack? It's a mess!
   Jack   I start**ed** to make a cake; then I decid**ed** to make a pizza. I cook**ed** all morning and clean**ed** all afternoon.
   Mum   You clean**ed**? What did you clean?
   Jack   My bedroom!

2. Say the past tense words with the /d/, /t/ and /ɪd/ endings.

3. 🔊 **5.04** Listen and repeat. Then practise with a partner.

UNIT 6
Stressed syllables in words

1. 🔊 **6.04** Listen to the sentences.

   Sarah's **fun**ny, **cheer**ful and **help**ful.
   Jonathan's **gen**erous, **con**fident and **tal**ented.
   E**liz**abeth's in**tel**ligent, ad**ven**turous and easy-**go**ing.

2. Say the two, three and four syllable words. Stress the words correctly.

3. 🔊 **6.05** Listen and repeat. Then practise with a partner.

PRONUNCIATION

UNIT 7
Vowel sounds: /ʊ/ and /uː/

1. 🔊 7.07 **Listen to the dialogue.**

   Luke Let's look in this room, Sue.
   Sue Wow! It's got things from the moon in it.
   Luke Look at these cool boots! I saw them in our science book.
   Sue We should take a photo for our school project, Luke.

2. Say the words with the short /ʊ/ vowel sound. Then say the words with the long /uː/ vowel sound.

3. 🔊 7.08 Listen and repeat. Then practise with a partner.

UNIT 8
Strong and weak forms of *was* and *were*

1. 🔊 8.02 **Listen to the dialogue.**

   Girl Was she shopping?
   Boy Yes, she was. She was shopping for socks.
   Girl Were they doing their homework?
   Boy No, they weren't. They were learning to surf!

2. Say the words with the /ɒ/ sound. Now say the words with the /ɜː/ sound. When *was* and *were* aren't stressed, we use the /ə/ sound. It's the same as /ɜː/ but shorter.

3. 🔊 8.03 Listen and repeat. Then practise with a partner.

UNIT 9
Vowel sounds: /ɪ/ and /aɪ/

1. 🔊 9.05 **Listen to the dialogue.**

   Jill I'd like to live in the wild. What about you, Mike?
   Mike I prefer a city lifestyle. I don't like lions or tigers – or insects!
   Jill But living in the wild's much more exciting!
   Mike Yes, Jill – and it's more frightening, too.

2. Say the words with the short /ɪ/ vowel sound. Then say the words with the long /aɪ/ vowel sound.

3. 🔊 9.06 Listen and repeat. Then practise with a partner.

UNIT 10
Voiced /ð/ and unvoiced /θ/ consonants

1. 🔊 10.04 **Listen to the dialogue.**

   Beth Look – there's the theatre.
   Harry That's not the right one, Beth.
   Beth Well, it says, 'The Fifth Avenue Theatre.'
   Harry But we want the one on Third Street!

2. Say the words with the voiced /ð/. Then say the words with the unvoiced /θ/.

3. 🔊 10.05 Listen and repeat. Then practise with a partner.

UNIT 11
The /h/ consonant sound

1. 🔊 11.02 **Listen to the dialogue.**

   Dr Harris Who's next? Oh, hello Harry. How can I help you?
   Harry Well, Dr Harris – my head's very hot!
   Dr Harris Let me see … does it hurt here?
   Harry Yes, doctor! That feels horrible!
   Dr Harris It's your hat, Harry. It's too small!

2. Say the words starting with the /h/ consonant sound.

3. 🔊 11.03 Listen and repeat. Then practise with a partner.

UNIT 12
Sentence stress

1. 🔊 12.03 **Listen to the stress in these sentences.**

   Car – plane – bike – train.
   A car, a plane, a bike, a train.
   A car and a plane and a bike and a train.
   A car and then a plane and then a bike and then a train.

2. Which words are stressed in every sentence? What happens to the other words?

3. 🔊 12.04 Listen and repeat. Then practise with a partner.

GET IT RIGHT!

UNIT 1
Adverbs of frequency

> Words like *sometimes, never, always* come <u>between</u> the subject and the verb or adjective.
> ✓ I **sometimes do** my homework on Saturday.
> ✗ I ~~do sometimes~~ my homework on Saturday.

Correct the six adverbs that are in the wrong place.

I have always fun on Saturday! In the morning, I usually meet my friends in the park or they come sometimes to my house. In the afternoon, we go often swimming. I never do homework on Saturday. In the evening, we have always pizza. My mum usually cooks the pizza at home, but we go occasionally to a restaurant. I always am very tired on Sunday!

like + *-ing*

> We use the *-ing* form of the verb after verbs expressing likes and dislikes.
> ✓ He **likes watching** TV.   ✗ He ~~likes watch~~ TV.

Find five mistakes in the conversation. Correct them.

Lucy   What do you like doing, Jim?
Jim   I love play with my dog, Spud.
Lucy   Does he enjoy swim?
Jim   No, he hates swim. But he likes go to the beach.
Lucy   I like play on the beach, too!

UNIT 2
Present continuous

> We form the present continuous with the present simple of *be* before the *-ing* form (e.g., *running, doing, wearing*, etc.) of the main verb, i.e., subject + *be* + *-ing* form of the verb.
> ✓ I **am looking** at the sky.
> ✗ ~~I looking~~ at the sky.
>
> But in questions, we use the present simple of *be* <u>before</u> the person doing the action, i.e., *be* + subject + *-ing* form of verb.
> ✓ Why **are you looking** at the sky?
> ✗ ~~Why you are looking~~ at the sky?

Put the correct form of *be* in the correct place in the sentences.

1 What you looking at?
2 They going shopping today.
3 I looking for a new jacket.
4 She wearing a beautiful dress.
5 Why he laughing? It's not funny!

Verbs of perception

> We use the present simple with verbs of perception (*look, taste, sound, smell*) to talk about something that is true now. We don't use the present continuous.
> ✓ His new jacket **looks terrible**!
> ✗ His new jacket ~~is looking terrible~~!
>
> We use *look, taste, sound, smell* + adjective, NOT *look, taste, sound, smell* + *like* + adjective.
> ✓ This pizza **tastes awful**!
> ✗ This pizza ~~tastes like awful~~!

Choose the correct sentence.

1 a I think this jacket looks expensive.
  b I think this jacket is looking expensive.
2 a Your weekend sounds great!
  b Your weekend sounds like great!
3 a Look at that dog. He looks like happy.
  b Look at that dog. He looks happy.
4 a The music is sounding beautiful.
  b The music sounds beautiful.

UNIT 3
much and *many*

> We use *many* with plural countable nouns and *much* with uncountable nouns.
> ✓ How **many** sandwiches have you got?
> ✗ How ~~much~~ sandwiches have you got?
> ✓ We haven't got **much** cheesecake.
> ✗ We haven't got ~~many~~ cheesecake.

Read the conversation. Choose *much* or *many*.

Sarah Hi, Julian, have we got everything we need for the party?
Julian We've got some crisps, but we haven't got ¹*many / much* fruit.
Sarah How ²*many / much* apples did you buy?
Julian We've got six apples, but we haven't got ³*many / much* vegetables.
Sarah I've got four tomatoes. How ⁴*many / much* people are coming?
Julian Everybody from our class is coming!
Sarah Oh, have we got ⁵*many / much* juice?
Julian Yes, but we haven't got ⁶*many / much* glasses.
Sarah Oh dear! We've got a problem.

too + adjective, (*not*) + adjective + *enough*

> We use *too* + adjective to say there is more than is necessary of something. We never use *too much* + adjective.
> ✓ The soup was **too cold**.
> ✗ The soup was *too much cold*.
>
> We use *not* before the adjective and *enough* **after** the adjective to say there is less than is necessary of something.
> ✓ The soup **wasn't hot enough**.
> ✗ The soup *wasn't enough hot*.

Write a cross (✗) next to the incorrect sentences. Then write the correct sentences.

1 We didn't go because the weather wasn't enough good.
    _____
2 The sausages were too spicy. And the pizza wasn't warm enough.
    _____
3 I didn't do my homework. I was too much tired.
    _____
4 The food he eats is healthy not enough.
    _____
5 The room wasn't enough big and the price was too much expensive.
    _____

UNIT 4
Possessive adjectives and pronouns

> We don't use *a/an* or *the* before possessive adjectives or possessive pronouns.
> ✓ This is **my sister**.
> ✗ This is *the my sister*.
> ✓ This is **mine**. Where is **yours**?
> ✗ This is *the mine*. Where is *the yours*?

Find five mistakes in the conversation. Correct them.

Clara Hi, Ben, is that your phone?
Ben No, it's a my brother's. His is black and the mine's blue. The one on the table is the mine.
Clara Oh, it's great! I need a new phone. The mine is really old!
Ben When is your birthday? Maybe your mum will give you a new phone.
Clara Hmm. But the my birthday is in December! I need a new phone now!

Possessive *'s*

> We don't usually use noun + *of* + noun to talk about possession. We use name or noun + *'s*.
> ✓ That is **my cousin's house**.
> ✗ That is *the house of my cousin*.

Rewrite these sentences using *'s*.

1 She's the sister of my best friend.
    _____
2 They are the grandparents of my cousin.
    _____
3 Is that the brother of your best friend?
    _____
4 She's the sister of my mum.
    _____
5 That's the phone of my brother.
    _____

UNIT 5
Modifiers: *quite, very, really*

> Remember: we use modifier + adjective (+ noun).
> We don't use noun + modifier + adjective.
> ✓ Pompeii has **a lot of very old buildings**.
> ✗ Pompeii has a lot of ~~buildings very old~~.
> ✓ The buildings are **very old**.
>
> Be careful when you write these words.
> - We write **quite** with the *e* **after** the *t*. Don't confuse **quite** with the adjective **quiet**.
>   - ✓ This chair is **quite** comfortable.
>   - ✗ This chair is ~~quiet~~ comfortable.
> - We write **really** with two **ll**s.
>   - ✓ Pompeii is **really** interesting.
>   - ✗ Pompeii is ~~realy~~ interesting.
> - We write **very** with one *r*.
>   - ✓ Their house is **very** big.
>   - ✗ Their house is ~~verry~~ big.

Find seven mistakes. Correct them.

We went to see our new house on Sunday. My dad wants to live near his office. It's realy annoying for me because a lot of my friends live near my house now. I was very sad when we went into the house. But when I saw inside it, I was amazed really! It looked quiet small, but inside it was really big. It had a kitchen really big and the bedrooms were verry big, too. But the best thing was the garden. It was beautiful really, with a swimming pool very big and lots of trees. I think my friends will like visiting my new house!

UNIT 6
Past simple (regular and irregular verbs)

> To make any verb negative in the past simple we use *didn't* + the base form of the verb. We don't use *didn't* + past simple. Remember to use the base form of regular and irregular verbs.
> ✓ We **didn't visit** the small house.
> ✗ We ~~didn't visited~~ the small house.

Choose the correct answer.

1. I'm sorry I didn't *come / came* to your party.
2. We didn't *went / go* on holiday last year.
3. I looked everywhere, but I didn't *found / find* my phone.
4. We visited the art gallery, but we didn't *see / saw* anything interesting.
5. We didn't *spend / spent* a lot of time in Paris. It was too hot!
6. I didn't *knew / know* you liked that band.

Double genitive

> We form the double genitive with noun + *of* + possessive pronoun (*mine, yours, his, hers, ours, yours, theirs*). We don't use object pronouns (*me, you, him, her, our, your, their*) to form the double genitive.
> ✓ She's **a friend of mine**.
> ✗ She's a friend ~~of me~~.
>
> We also form the double genitive with noun + *of* + possessive adjective (*my, your, his, her, our, your, their*) + noun + possessive *'s*.
> ✓ She's **a friend of my sister's**.
> ✗ She's a friend ~~of my sister~~.

Choose the correct answer.

1. Lisa is a good friend of *me / my / mine*.
2. Matt Damon is a favourite actor of my *sister / sister's*.
3. My brother went to the cinema with a friend of *him / he's / his*.
4. I met a cousin of *Rory's / Rory* at the party.
5. She brought a new classmate of *hers / her / she's* to the party.
6. Isn't that woman a teacher of *your / you / yours*?

UNIT 7
have to / don't have to

> We always use the base form of the verb after *have to / don't have to*.
> ✓ He **has to tidy** his room today.
> ✗ He has to ~~tidied~~ his room today.
> ✗ He has to ~~tidying~~ his room today.
>
> We use the correct form of *do + not/n't + have to* to say that something isn't necessary. We don't use *haven't to*.
> ✓ You **don't have to help** me. I can do it.
> ✗ You ~~haven't to~~ help me. I can do it.

Find six mistakes. Correct them.

I have to do a lot of housework at home, but I'm OK about that. I have to tidying my room, but I haven't to vacuum the floor. My brother has to does that. We have to do the washing up, but we don't have do the washing. My dad does that once a week. I haven't to do the cooking – my mum likes cooking. She says it helps her to relax. Of course, I have to doing my homework every day after school. I'm not OK about that!

UNIT 8
Past continuous vs. past simple

> We use the past continuous to talk about background actions in the past, and the past simple for actions which happened at one moment in the past.
> ✓ I **was watching** television when the lights **went** out.
> ✗ I ~~watched~~ television when the lights went out.

Complete the story with the past continuous or past simple of the verb in brackets.

The surprise!

It ¹_____ (happen) last Saturday while I ² _____ (have) a party at my house. At 9 o'clock, we ³_____ (dance) and having a fantastic time. Then, suddenly, the lights ⁴_____ (go) out. I ⁵_____ (close) my eyes and screamed! But when I ⁶_____ (stop), I heard that all my friends ⁷_____ (laugh). When I ⁸_____ (open) my eyes, everybody was smiling at me. When my mum ⁹_____ (arrive) with a cake and candles, I finally understood …

UNIT 9
Comparative adjectives

> We use *more* + adjective with two syllables or more to form the comparative. We don't use *more* with adjectives with one syllable or with adjectives that are already in the comparative form (e.g. *smaller, colder, friendlier*).
> ✓ His room is **smaller** than mine.
> ✗ His room is ~~more small~~ than mine.
> ✗ His room is ~~more smaller~~ than mine.

Choose the correct sentence.

1. a Lions can run more faster during the night.
   b Lions can run faster during the night.
2. a The weather in the Kalahari is drier than in Europe.
   b The weather in the Kalahari is more dry than in Europe.
3. a It's more hotter in the summer than in the winter.
   b It's hotter in the summer than in the winter.
4. a People in the countryside are friendlier than people in the city.
   b People in the countryside are more friendlier than people in the city.

can / can't for ability

> We always use the base form of the verb after *can / can't*.
> ✓ He **can swim**, but he **can't surf**.
> ✗ He can ~~swam~~, but he can't ~~to surf~~.

Choose the correct verb form.

1. I love living by the sea. On sunny days, I can *went / going / go* to the beach.
2. On cold days, you can *do / doing / to do* the shopping in the town centre.
3. We can *learning / learn / to learn* a lot about wildlife from nature programmes.
4. You can't *drive / driving / drove* a car if you're 15.
5. They can't *to come / coming / come* to the party because they're on holiday.

UNIT 10
be going to for intentions

> We use the present tense of *be* + *going to* + base form of the verb to talk about our intentions in the future. Remember to use the present tense of *be*.
> ✓ He *is going to study* all weekend.
> ✗ He *going* to study all weekend.

Complete the sentences with *be going to* and the verb in brackets.

1 He _____ (paint) his bedroom on Saturday.
2 I've bought a new chair. I _____ (put) it near the TV.
3 We _____ (visit) my cousin because he is ill.
4 They _____ (go) to the sports centre by car.
5 We _____ (watch) a film tonight.

Present continuous for arrangements

> We use the present continuous to talk about arrangements for the future. We don't use the present simple.
> ✓ I'm *going to visit* my grandparents tomorrow.
> ✗ I *go* to visit my grandparents tomorrow.
>
> To ask questions about arrangements, we use question word + *be* + subject + the *-ing* form of the verb. Remember to put the words in the correct order.
> ✓ What *are you doing* tomorrow?
> ✗ What *you are doing* tomorrow?

Find six mistakes in the dialogue. Correct them.

Lara Hi, Sam, what you are doing on Saturday?
Sam   Well, in the morning, I play football in the park.
Lara What are you doing in the afternoon?
Sam   I don't do anything. What are you doing?
Lara I paint my bedroom.
Sam   Cool! What colour do you use?
Lara I'm going to choose the colour when I go to the shop.
Sam   Which shop are you going to?
Lara I go to the shop in the high street at 2 o'clock.
Sam   OK. I'll meet you there! I can help you to choose.

UNIT 11
will / won't for future predictions

> We use the present continuous to talk about things happening now and future arrangements. We use *will* or *won't* + base form to make future predictions.
> ✓ I'm sure you*'ll do* well in your test next week.
> ✗ I'm sure you *are doing* well in your test next week.
> ✓ I*'m going* to a party on Saturday.
> ✗ I *will go* to a party on Saturday.

Choose present continuous or 'll / won't to complete the email.

Gareth
gareth@email.co.uk

Holiday!

Hi Gareth,
I don't think ¹*I'll see / I'm seeing* you before my holiday. ²*We'll leave / We're leaving* on Saturday, so ³*I'm being / I'll be* very busy. ⁴*I'll go / I'm going* shopping on Friday, so ⁵*I'm not being / I won't be* at art class. ⁶*I'll need / I'm needing* to buy some shorts – my dad says ⁷*it'll be / it's being* really hot in Tunisia! ⁸*I'll phone / I'm phoning* you on Friday night if I have time. I have to go now. ⁹*I'll help / I'm helping* my sister with her homework.
Marcus

UNIT 12
Present perfect simple

> We use the present perfect simple to talk about situations or actions that happened at some time in the past.
> ✓ I *have met* a lot of famous actors.
> ✗ I *met* a lot of famous actors.
>
> We use the past simple to talk about situations or actions at a specific time in the past.
> ✓ A year ago, I *met* a famous actor.
> ✗ A year ago, I *have met* a famous actor.

Find seven mistakes in the text. Correct them.

My parents work for international companies, so I travelled a lot. I've lived in Europe, Asia and the US. Two years ago, I have lived in Spain for six months. My brother's only three, so he only went to Europe and he forgot that trip! My dad travelled to more places. He has been to Australia and New Zealand last year, but we never visited England.

STUDENT A

UNIT 2, PAGE 23

Student A
1 You are a customer in a sports shop. You like a pair of trainers.
   You want a black pair.
   You want to know the price.
   You want to try them on.
2 You are an assistant in a clothes shop. Student B likes a sweatshirt. It's €36.95. You have green, blue or red.

UNIT 5, PAGE 54

Student A
You and your friend have got £200. You are at a flea market buying furniture for a new room for your youth club. These are the prices of the pieces of furniture:
- 2 armchairs £30
- cooker £20
- shelf £5
- table with 8 chairs £70
- desk and lamp £25
- sofa £75
- large carpet £70
- mirror £10
- wardrobe £30
- small carpet £30
- sofa £40
- 8 posters of film stars £5

You want to buy the 2 armchairs, the large carpet, the cooker and the posters.
You do not want to buy the shelf or the wardrobe.
You are uncertain about the table with the 8 chairs and the sofas.
Have a conversation and agree on what to buy.

UNIT 7, PAGE 72

Student A
You are a son or daughter. You are at home.
You want to see a friend.
You are phoning your mum or dad about it.
When your mum/dad tells you that you should do some housework, ask her/him what you have to do.
Also, tell your mum/dad that there are some things she/he shouldn't forget. When she/he asks you what things, say:
She/He …
- should do the shopping
- shouldn't be late tonight (you want to watch a film together with her/him)
- mustn't forget to bring some chocolate biscuits!

The line is not very good, so you have to ask your mum or dad several times to repeat what she/he has said.

UNIT 11, PAGE 105

Student A
1 You are a patient and Student B is a doctor. Choose one of the pictures here. Tell Student B about your problem. Have the conversation.
2 Now Student B is the patient and you are the doctor. Ask Student B about their problem. Have the conversation.

STUDENT B

UNIT 2, PAGE 23

Student B
1. You are an assistant in a sports shop.
   Student A likes a pair of trainers. They're €34.99.
   You only have brown or red (not black).
2. You are a customer in a clothes shop. You like a sweatshirt.
   You want a green one.
   You want to know the price.
   You want to try it on.

UNIT 5, PAGE 54

Student B
You and your friend have got £200. You are at a flea market buying furniture for a new room for your youth club. These are the prices of the pieces of furniture:
- 2 armchairs £30
- cooker £20
- shelf £5
- table with 8 chairs £70
- desk and lamp £25
- sofa £75
- large carpet £70
- mirror £10
- wardrobe £30
- small carpet £30
- sofa £40
- 8 posters of film stars £5

You want to buy the table with the 8 chairs, the cooker, the large carpet and one of the sofas.
You do not want to buy the 2 armchairs or the posters.
You are uncertain about the desk and the lamp.
Have a conversation and agree on what to buy.

UNIT 7, PAGE 72

Student B
You are a mum or dad. Your son/daughter is phoning you.
Make sure he/she knows that he/she has to do some housework before he/she can go out. When he/she asks you, say:
He/She …
- has to tidy up his/her room
- should load the dishwasher
- mustn't forget to vacuum the floor

When your son or daughter tells you that there are things you shouldn't forget, ask them what things.
The line is not very good, so you have to ask your son or daughter several times to repeat what he/she has said.

UNIT 11, PAGE 105

Student B
1. You are a doctor and Student A is a patient. Ask Student A about their problem. Have the conversation.
2. Now you are the patient and Student A is the doctor. Choose one of the pictures here. Tell the doctor about your problem. Have the conversation.